Library
history

OUTLINES OF MODERN LIBRARIANSHIP

Titles included in the series are

Children's librarianship
Local studies librarianship
Special librarianship
Book production
Library history
Current awareness services
Cataloguing
Music librarianship
History and theory of classification
Practical reference work
Public library administration
Medical librarianship

OUTLINES OF MODERN LIBRARIANSHIP

Library history

James G Ollé

CLIVE BINGLEY LONDON

K G SAUR MUNICH · NEW YORK · PARIS

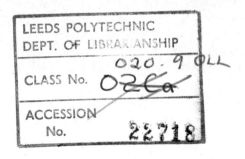
First published 1979
by Clive Bingley Ltd
Set in 11 on 12 point Baskerville by Allset
Printed and bound in the UK by
Redwood Burn Ltd Trowbridge and Esher
Copyright © 1979 James G Ollé
ISBN: 0-85157-271-5

Clive Bingley Ltd
Commonwealth House, New Oxford Street, London WC1

K G Saur Verlag
P O Box 71 10 09, D-8000 Munich 71

K G Saur Publishing Inc
175 Fifth Avenue, New York NY 10010

K G Saur Editeur
38 rue de Bassano, F-75008 Paris

British Library Cataloguing in Publication Data

Olle, James Gordon
  Library history.-(Outlines of
  modern librarianship).
  1. Libraries-Great Britain-
     Historiography
  2. Libraries-United States-
     Historiography
  I. Title   II Series
  021'. 0072'041   Z791.A1

ISBN 0-85157-271-5

CONTENTS

PREFACE

THIS IS neither an invitation to, nor a defence of library history. Neither seems to be necessary now. Nor is it a guide to the literature of library history for examination students. This I have already endeavoured to provide in my *Library history : an examination guidebook* (2nd revised edition, Clive Bingley, 1971). Instead, I have tried to define the present state of library history. This, I think, is a proper exercise, as enough work has been done on library history to call for a general survey of what has been accomplished; and also, what is just as important, some indication of what has yet to be done.

In restricting my study to the library history of Britain and the USA, I mean no disrespect to other countries who have made their own contributions to library development and are well aware of it; I am merely working within the safe limitations of my own knowledge and recognising that, in Britain and the USA a considerable amount of work has been done in the cause of library history, and that the development of library history studies in the two countries has been roughly parallel. I believe, however, that my general observations on library history are of universal application.

Although I hope that this book will interest library history students, more particularly because their historical studies are commonly supported by written exercises of one kind or another, it has been designed to appeal to anyone with an interest in library history.

I have said little about the teaching of library history, for the simple reason that I have been a library school lecturer long enough to know that it is useless to pontificate about either syllabuses or teaching methods. A syllabus is a propitiation to an academic board. Its one essential feature is that it should be wide enough to move around in, but there should be no intention, or obligation, to cover all of it. As to teaching methods, as the head of my department is fond of telling us, a good teacher teaches from strength, and strengths differ. The communication of knowledge follows the communication of enthusiasm. One teacher is only happy with the full panoply of audio-visual aids; another needs only a stick of chalk, or the shade of a friendly palm.

It would have been against the purpose of this book had I turned it into a narrative bibliography of library history. Of necessity, I have had to be highly selective in my examples, and the lack of a reference to any particular book, article, thesis, or dissertation does not necessarily mean that I am unaware of it, or do not rate it highly.

I have two regrets. The first is that when I completed my manuscript, the promised *American library history: a bibliography* had not been published. I have no doubt it will give American library history studies a prime aid and a new impetus. My second regret is that British and American librarians should take so little interest in each other's library history. After all, there are several strong links between the two, links through shared experiences in bibliothecal and bibliographical activities, through collaboration in cataloguing codes and in the common use of classification schemes; and, perhaps most interesting of all, through the Anglo-American interests and activities of librarians such as Melvil Dewey and Eric Moon, and library benefactors such as Thomas Bray and Andrew Carnegie. It should not be forgotten, either, that American librarians were present, in force, at the birth of the Library Association of the United Kingdom, as it was called in its early days; and that the *Library journal* was, for a while, the official journal of both the American Library Association and the Library Association. How the two countries compare in their interest and achievements in library history, the following pages, I hope, will show.

Strangely, although we are all specialists nowadays, every qualified librarian thinks he is a 'complete librarian'. I have long believed that a knowledge of library history, and the possession of an unwavering pride in the library profession, which library history amply sustains, are a part of that completeness.

Unless otherwise stated, the place of publication of all books mentioned in the text is London. For full details of the *Encyclopedia of library and information science* and the journals *Library history* and the *Journal of library history*, all of which are frequently cited, see the classified bibliography of reference aids in library history in chapter six.

JAMES G OLLÉ
Department of Library and Information Studies,
Loughborough University of Technology,
England.

Postscript to preface
Since the above preface was written, the promised *American library history: a bibliography* has been published. (For details see p93.)

We still await a definitive history of the ALA, but a useful tentative history, based on a doctoral dissertation, is now available: Dennis Thomison *A history of the American Library Association 1876-1972* (Chicago: American Library Association, 1978).

JGO

ONE

INTRODUCTION: THE STATE OF THE ART

AMONG the most ardent defenders of library history, under-
standably, are the leading library historians. Among them is
Raymond Irwin, who said, 'If all that interests the young
librarian is a bread and butter wage as a technician, then
there is little in history that he need bother about.'(1)

W A Munford's thoughts were moving on a similar plane
when he said that one way of judging the maturity of a profession would be to consider how much pride it takes in its
own history.(2) Judging by the volume of literature on
library history, the library profession takes a considerable
pride in its past. But, as we shall see, not everyone is prepared to accept this deduction.

II

Putting aside, for the present, the question 'Is library history
of any real importance?', let us turn to another question
somewhat easier to resolve: 'How has the literature of library
history reached its present state?' Richard Krzys tried to
answer this in his essay 'Library historiography' in the
Encyclopedia of library and information science.(3) The
result is disappointing, partly because Krzys concerns himself
more with the ancient roots of the subject than its modern
branches, and partly because his dry analytical approach to
library history leaves the reader with little inclination to
explore it further.

By contrast, Jesse H Shera's 'The literature of American
library history', published originally in the *Library quarterly*
January 1945, and reprinted, in expanded form, in his
volume of collected essays *Knowing books and men; knowing
computers, too* (Littleton, Colo, 1973, Libraries Unlimited) is

informative, sensible and of much more than passing interest. Recently it has been supplemented, usefully, though not so magisterially, by John Calvin Colson in 'The writing of American library history, 1876-1976' *Library trends* 25 (1) July 1976, 7-21. There are no comparable studies of the development of British library history; but if there were, they would show an almost parallel development. That is to say, the emergence of library history in the mid-nineteenth century as chronicle history, and its belated coming of age in the present century, first in America and later in Britain, as what Professor Shera calls 'true history', history which involves synthesis and the evaluation and interpretation of relationships, and not just a bare recital of isolated facts.

III

Edward Edwards (1812-1886) has been called the father of the public library movement. There are grounds for calling him, also, the father of library history, in that he was the first writer to specialise in it and the first to bring it some measure of recognition as a subject worthy of attention.

Edwards's contribution to the literature of library history is scarcely believable. Despite a sketchy education, and an unfortunate professional career, marred by disputes, dismissals and financial worries, Edwards somehow contrived to write more on library history than anyone before or since. The product of his labours was a series of massive volumes which still impress; even though, in many a library, their pages are brittle through lack of use. In order of publication they are: *Memoirs of libraries* (two volumes, 1859), *Libraries and founders of libraries* (1864), *Free town libraries* (1869) and *Lives of the founders of the British Museum* (1870). In his retirement, Edwards laboured on a revised edition of the *Memoirs*. The fragment he wrote and had printed was bound and distributed, in 1901, by Thomas Greenwood, his first biographer.

Edward Edwards's prime misfortune was that he was born into the wrong class and in the wrong century. A man of scholarly inclinations, he was denied the kind of education which would have given him the opportunity of scholarly pursuits and the benefits of scholarly discipline. He was the

12

son of a small-time London builder and he acquired his learning from such libraries as he could use, an expedient which turned his mind in the direction of a public library service supported from local taxation.

Edwards was obliged to work strenuously for his living, except for the early years when he was fortunate enough to be employed as a supernumerary assistant in the British Museum Library, and his work brought him only occasional satisfaction. It is remarkable that he should have written so much; regrettable that he should have had to write under such difficulties and with such little reward.

As a library historian, Edwards was ambitious and untiring, but his work always left something to be desired. In the words of Richard Garnett, who wrote the perceptive article about him in the *Dictionary of national biography*, 'he was erudite and industrious though not sufficiently discriminating'. He attempted too many subjects and dealt with each of them at inordinate length. His heavy reliance on secondary resources was something he could not help, as he had too little opportunity to travel; but, even so, he transcribed when he should have abstracted, and in the face of informed criticism he was resentful when he should have been apologetic. Except in small doses, his books are unreadable. Ironically, he was at his best when he said what libraries should do, rather than what they had done. Had he only set his mind to it, he could have given his generation what it most needed—a first-rate practical manual on library economy, but history always got in the way.

After Edwards, the literature of library history grew slowly in Britain. The new periodicals of librarianship which came into existence in the latter part of the nineteenth century published occasional articles of historical interest, but books on library history were few. At the turn of the century John Willis Clark, University Registary at Cambridge, had a modest and well-deserved success with his history of classical and mediaeval library planning and architecture, in a well researched monograph called *The care of books* (2nd edition, Cambridge University Press, 1902). A few years ago, P S Morrish carefully assessed this work in 'John Willis Clark revisited: aspects of early modern library design' *Library history* 3(3) Spring 1974, 87-107, and decided that, despite its original faults, and the corrections which need to be made to it in the light of later research, it is still useful as a starting point for serious students.

A few years after Clark's near masterpiece, Ernest A Savage, a public librarian with a nimbler mind and better judgment than Edward Edwards, besides superior literary talent, wrote quickly, one after the other, *The story of libraries and book-collecting* (Routledge, [1909]) and *Old English libraries* (Methuen, 1911). The former was little more than an up-dated abstract of Edward Edwards's *Memoirs*, but the latter was a substantial, ambitious work, which involved Savage in more research than he had bargained for. Both books were well received, but Savage was well aware that they could have been better had they been written under more favourable conditions. He was also annoyed by the fact that neither work, after expenses had been paid, made him any money; but this is still not an unusual circumstance in the field of library history.

What might have been the most notable achievement of the inter-war years, John Minto *A history of the public library movement in Great Britain and Ireland* (Allen & Unwin, 1932) turned out to be little more than a legislative history, coupled with a summary history of the various library associations. The most durable works of the period were two specialised histories, widely different in everything except their mastery of their subjects: Burnett Hillman Streeter *The chained library: a survey of four centuries in the evolution of the English library* (Macmillan, 1931), which was inspired by the author's work of restoration at the library of Hereford Cathedral; and R C Barrington Partridge *The history of the legal deposit of books throughout the British Empire* (Library Association, 1938), a novel venture into library history which yielded more of interest than most readers expected.

It was not until after World War II, with a far more prosperous and rapidly expanding library world, that library history became a recognised subject for study and research in Britain. During the 1960's it became a feature of the syllabuses of the library schools, and the same decade brought the first wave of library history theses. (At first these were mainly Fellowship theses of the Library Association; now the balance is more in favour of the universities.)

Readily discernible in the records of all library history activities in Britain since World War II is the genial figure of W A Munford, Director General of the National Library for the Blind, who has somehow found time to assume the additional roles of library historian, supervisor of library history theses and dissertations, and instigator and chairman of the Library Association Library History Group.

As a library historian, Dr Munford's greatest achievements have been his biography *Edward Edwards, 1812-1886: portrait of a librarian* (Library Association, 1963) and his centennial *History of the Library Association 1877-1977* (Library Association, 1976); but he is probably still best known for his little volume on British public library history, which he called *Penny rate* (Library Association, 1951), the first book on the subject to firmly draw the boundaries of it, and the first book on library history to enjoy a wide sale.

Raymond Irwin's preference in writing library history was the essay, or rather the lecture, as it was as lectures that most of his essays on library history came into being. The majority were collected in two companion volumes: *The heritage of the English library* (Allen & Unwin, 1964) and *The origins of the English library* (Allen & Unwin, 1958) which was re-named, in its second and enlarged edition, *The English library* (Allen & Unwin 1966). Irwin wrote not only with knowledge and enthusiasm, but with the urbanity of an Edwardian belletrist, a characteristic he held in common with his learned contemporary Arundell Esdaile, who wrote too little on library history.

But with the advent of Thomas Kelly, in the 1960's, British library history assumed a breadth and depth which it had not reached before. Dr Kelly is not a librarian, but an educationist and a well-known authority on the history and bibliography of adult education. After working for a while as a schoolmaster he became an educational editor with the Scottish publishing firm of W & R Chambers, then a university lecturer in adult education and finally Professor of

15

Adult Education at the University of Liverpool. He is now, in his nominal retirement, Professor Emeritus.

Professor Kelly's interest in library history arose from his work on the history of adult education, which included a fine biography of George Birkbeck, with which was combined a history of the early years of the mechanics' institutes. By a happy chance, his interest in the history of libraries was stimulated and directed by the Library Association, which commissioned him to write a new history of the public library movement in Great Britain. Professor Kelly asked if he might first trace the history of the predecessors of the rate-supported public library. Hence, we now have two complementary works which have not only been widely praised, but widely read: *Early public libraries: a history of public libraries in Great Britain before 1850* (Library Association, 1966) and *History of public libraries in Great Britain 1845-1975* (2nd edition, Library Association, 1977). The former brought together, for the first time, details of many libraries whose existence had scarcely been realised; the latter brought under control an extraordinary amount of published and unpublished information on the British public library movement, so that for the first time we could really see what it had achieved, despite the hindrances of inadequate funds, an unsatisfactory local government structure, confusion over the purpose of public libraries, and a far greater variation in local circumstances than previous historians had recognised. By virtue of his knowledge of educational history, Professor Kelly was able to place public libraries in their social context; and the careful documentation of his work gave future researchers instant aid in their own exploration of the source literature.

The 1960's also saw the establishment, in 1962, of the Library Association Library History Group, whose purpose is to unite members of the Library Association interested in library history through meetings, discussions and publications. Latterly, its meetings have found less favour with its members than its publications, in particular its half-yearly journal *Library history*, first published in 1967. The Group has also been responsible for three volumes of the highly efficient *British library history: bibliography*. (For details of these publications see chapter six.)

IV

According to Jesse H Shera, library history began in the USA with Josiah Quincy's *History of the Boston Athenaeum* (1851). It also had a place in the classic report of the US Bureau of Education's *Public libraries in the United States of America (1876)*; in fact, according to Professor Shera, the historical approach was 'inherent in the editorial plan'. Thereafter, the literature of library history grew in volume, but without gaining much in quality. As Shera puts it, 'library history writing became broader but not much deeper'.

In 1931, Arnold K Borden, a Harvard student, published an essay called 'The sociological beginnings of the library movement' *Library quarterly* I (3) July 1931, 278-282. It dealt briefly with the influences on the development of libraries in America, over the previous century, and it concluded with the observation: 'From the point of view of history, as well as from that of contemporary conditions, the library needs to be studied in the light of sociology, economics, and other branches of human knowledge.'

The idea, if not the practice, of studying the history of libraries in their social context is commonplace now, but it had some novelty then. Borden's article was noticed and remembered by Jesse Shera when he set to work on his well-known doctoral dissertation, *Foundations of the public library: the origins of the public library movement in New England 1629-1855* (Chicago: University of Chicago Press, 1948). With this work, and another 'broadly conceived' history (to use his own phrase) by Sidney Ditzion, *Arsenals of a democratic culture: a social history of the American public library movement in New England and the Middle States from 1850 to 1900* (Chicago: American Library Association, 1947) library history achieved a maturity and sense of purpose in the USA about twenty years before it did so in Great Britain. What Shera and Ditzion were trying to do was discussed by Ditzion, some years later, in 'The research and writing of library history', one of a series of papers written in honour of Jesse Shera published under the title *Toward a theory of librarianship* edited by Conrad H Rawski (Metuchen NJ: Scarecrow Press, 1973).

To the USA also, and not Great Britain, goes the credit of establishing the first society devoted to library history. The

American Library History Round Table was approved by the ALA Council in December 1946 and held its first meeting at the ALA Conference of 1947. The Round Table exists to provide a forum for library history, which it does mainly through meetings. Since 1961, there have been several Seminars in Library History in the USA, of which the Round Table has been a co-sponsor. Presumably, because of its accent on meetings rather than publications, the membership of the Round Table is only about a third of that of the Library Association Library History Group, which is now just over a thousand.

A plea for a means of communication 'within the library and history professions', made by Professor Richard A Bartlett at the Second Library History Seminar, March 1965, bore fruit. The first issue of the quarterly *Journal of library history* appeared in January 1966. Like its British counterpart, *Library history*, it soon justified its existence and is now firmly established and indispensable.

According to Professor John C Colson, since 1945, the year in which Jesse Shera published his survey of the development of American library history, some 140 full-length works on various aspects of library history have been published. A few, at least, are worthy successors to the landmark volumes of Shera and Ditzion.

V

One undoubtedly good result of the growing interest in library history has been the particular attention which has been paid to the bibliographical control of the literature on it. Although the *Journal of library history* inaugurated a 'Year's work in American library history' feature in 1968, the first major attempt to list the literature of library history was made by the Library Association Library History Group with its *British library history: bibliography 1962-1968* (Library Association, 1972) and its successor *British library history: bibliography 1969-1972* (Library Association, 1975). The first volume covered seven years and mustered 820 entries; the second volume covered only four years but mustered 746 entries. By the 1960's, it would seem, library history was in a healthy state in Britain. But was it?

A close analysis of the entries in these two volumes leads one to conclude that most of the writings on British library history have been small-scale and many of them unpremeditated. By small-scale I mean that often they have been pamphlets, sections of monographs, or contributions to reference works, symposia, periodicals, or newspapers. By unpremeditated I mean that some writings have been the by-product of other investigations into history. For example, an academic commissioned to write the history of his university devotes a part of his text to the university library. Then there are obituaries and other items written by request, and at short notice, such as anniversary articles.

There are also theses and dissertations. (Terminology is irregular for these. When I speak of dissertations I have in mind doctoral theses and dissertations.) They are hardly unpremeditated, but they are characteristic of most contributions to library history in that they are often their authors' only contributions. This phenomenon has already been noted by Michael H Harris, who, in the course of his critical survey of 'Two years' work in American library history, 1969-1970' *Journal of library history* 7 (1) January 1972, tempered his enthusiasm for the good work which had been done by saying:

'A glance at the [bibliographical] notes to this essay indicates a rather discouraging trend: few of the authors cited here are serious library historians. A large proportion of the significant work was originally prepared in partial fulfillment of the requirements for graduate degrees, and their authors—now that the degrees are earned—have taken administrative or teaching positions which leave little or no time for further research in this area. Other work has been done by talented individuals who have made a single foray into the field of historical research without entertaining any thought of further work. As a result we see too little cumulation of skill, experience, knowledge, and maturity in library historians. Library history remains by and large, like the Library History Round Table, a playground for amateurs.' (p 45)

I think some, at least, of the 'once-for-all' American library historians covered by this lament would stoutly affirm that they had, for a while, been perfectly serious. But it is unfortunate that, in the writing of library history, the value of cumulated experience is seldom felt.

Not surprisingly, interest in library history is much the same on both sides of the Atlantic: only a few librarians are continuously interested and the rest occasionally so. I have heard some librarians declare, quite frankly, that they have no interest in library history at all. This I find hard to believe. A man may no more detach himself from the history of his profession than he may detach himself from the history of his family, town, country or religion. This may mean no more than an occasional curiosity about it, but a real liking, if only a quiescent liking, is probably never entirely absent. Recently a colleague said to me, 'I never read biographies of librarians. But I wouldn't mind reading a life of J P' (a remarkable chief librarian for whom he had once worked).

There is one difference between the state of library history in Britain and the USA. In the USA, notwithstanding the considerable achievements of the post-war years, there is a far greater tendency among those librarians who do care for library history to bemoan the fact that there are other librarians who do not. Thus, Michael H Harris, in the introduction to his admirable anthology *Reader in American library history* (New York: NCR Microcard Editions, 1971) said: 'In general, the American librarian has not been concerned with library history. The pressures of day to day library administration have left little time to plan for the future, let alone contemplate the past.' John C Colson, in his 'Speculations on the uses of library history' *Journal of library history* 4 (1) January 1969, 65-71 said, 'Our profession has been largely indifferent to the need for a better understanding of history. It has regarded history as an ornament which is nice to have on the edifice, but really not very useful.' Viewed from this side of the Atlantic, the state of library history in the USA does not seem all that discouraging.

VI

Towards the end of his life, Ernest A Savage reflected on his involvement with library history in a reminiscent essay called 'Casual amateur in bibliography' *Library Association record*

65(10) October 1963, 361-365. Recalling the difficulties he encountered when writing his two books, at the beginning of the century, he said 'The study of library history must be subsidised and supervised'.

Thanks to the proliferation of library schools, there is now a good deal of supervision, but financial help for research in library history is still rare, especially in Great Britain.

As mentioned earlier, theses and dissertations in library history were scarcely known in Britain before the 1960's. In the USA they have a longer history, although, as Michael H Harris has shown, in his bibliography of graduate research in library history in the USA, *A guide to research in American library history* (2nd edition, Metuchen NJ: Scarecrow Press, 1974), the majority have been written since 1950.

Although this growth in library history research is welcome, some of the work done shows a minimum of scholarship and much of it a lack of literary grace. As to the latter point, writing a thesis or a dissertation carries with it an obligation to observe certain conventions. The emotional temperature must be kept low and almost every fact must be secured to a footnote. There is even a kind of thesis jargon, intended, one must suppose, to lend an air of erudition to an otherwise plain, unvarnished narrative, often reinforced by the kind of observations which a former chief of mine liked to call 'a magnificent glimpse of the obvious'.

There are exceptions, of course. Several excellent published histories began as dissertations, among them W A Munford *Edward Edwards 1812-1886* (Library Association, 1963), *W B Aitken A history of the public library movement in Scotland to 1955* (Glasgow: Scottish Library Association, 1971), George S Bobinski *Carnegie libraries: their history and impact on American public library development* (Chicago: American Library Association, 1969) and the books by Jesse H Shera and Sidney Ditzion mentioned earlier.

When all reservations have been made about formal academic research in library history, it must be admitted that it has given us several works of inestimable value.

It should be added, also, that sometimes the subject of a dissertation has an inherent liveliness which refuses to be suppressed by the conventions of the dissertation formula. For illustration one may take those British towns (they include a notorious group of London metropolitan boroughs) where the fight to establish a public library service was long and remarkably bitter. If you have ever doubted whether brewers and publicans really did oppose the adoption of the Public Library Acts, through fear of losing custom, or whether the provision of a public library service could be a fierce and protracted subject of debate between rival political parties, then the public library history of the former metropolitan boroughs of St Marylebone and St Pancras will surprise you. No historian, providing he quotes freely from the original records, could make this kind of history dull.

VII

Nevertheless, it cannot be denied that much of the literature of library history is dull. The dullness is never absolute. There is no theme, no event, in the entire spectrum of history which is not of potential interest to some reader, however glumly it may be recorded. But it is particularly difficult, in library history, to stimulate wide interest.

Before I joined the library profession, I had a vague notion, still widely held, I think, that if there was any type of institution in the civilised world where life was still life, quite devoid of the stresses and passions which prevailed elsewhere, it was a library. I soon discovered otherwise. Chronic poverty, ignorance of the principles of management, the lack of approved standards, and lingering doubts as to what purpose they were meant to fulfil, made many of the libraries of my youth uneasy places to work in. There has been substantial improvement since World War II, but human nature never sheds its idiosyncrasies; chief librarians and their staffs and committees will always be liable to fall out of gear, and new ideas will always be suspect by some, and old ones by others. In short, in librarianship, as in every human activity, progress will never be as smooth as a billiard table, or as straight as a Roman road. Unfortunately, much of the literature of library history is serenely oblivious of its human aspect. Notable chiefs and benefactors are given their due,

22

more or less; *they* can hardly be avoided. But these apart, one is likely to be living in the stifling world of statistical aggregates.

Gradually, I believe, things are changing for the better; we are beginning to realise that a remote and frigid view of library history will never do. But, like most professions, we have been reluctant to see ourselves in print as we see ourselves in life.

VIII

Analysing my own knowledge of library history, I find that it is compounded of three elements: what I have experienced, what I have heard and what I have read. The second element is, in some ways, the most interesting. Unfortunately, it is of the least use. Even though it may be true, it is often difficult to verify, beyond reasonable doubt, and it is usually difficult to publish without causing anger or distress.

Nevertheless, some of the stories I have heard about the old-style patriarchal chief librarians of the past probably deserve a place somewhere in the margin of library history, if only for their amusement value. For a taste: there was the librarian who, entertained too lavishly by a bookseller at the Library Association's annual conference, spent all his book-fund in a few hazy minutes and eked out the rest of the year in miserable penitence. There was the librarian who thought the best place in the world to grow mushrooms was the basement of his central library; the librarian who was so nervous of meeting any of his readers that he always remained in his office, which he could reach by a private staircase; and the librarian who, dressed in loud checks, like a raffish book-maker, one night unknowingly accosted one of his own assistants, under the lambent lights of the Town Hall Square, thinking she was a prostitute. These, you may say, are trivia, but they are part of life's ingredients, nevertheless.

To some readers, I suspect, the reality of library history is all the more suspect because there is no humour in it. But humour was always there, although, perhaps, unrecognisable at the time. I can well believe that the pre-war public library which despatched overdue notices to one part of the city

23

addressed 'Mr', and to the rest of the city addressed 'Esq', honestly thought it was observing a nice point of etiquette.

But one of the oddest examples of humour in library history concerns the literature of library history itself. When Dr W A Munford was trying to find a publisher for his biography of William Ewart, the worthy Member of Parliament who supported the British public library movement in its crucial pioneering days, one offered to publish it if the author 'would liven it up and give Ewart some sex life'. 'Why not', he asked, 'give him a mistress, living, say, in St John's Wood?.'(4)

An exquisite example of humour in library history is to be found in a charming essay by Caroline E Werkley, 'Mr Carnegie's "Libary"' *Journal of library history* 4 (2) April 1969, 142-151, which recalls the early days of the Carnegie Library at Moberly, Missouri, where Mrs Werkley's mother was librarian. 'Mother's—and Mr Carnegie's—library was a square, solid gray stone building, with pillars and pigeons decorating its front.' Mother looked upon the Moberly library (or 'libary', as its readers called it) as Mr Carnegie's personal property, and Mr Carnegie himself as a saintly figure, a judgment which was by no means universally held, as Mother knew. 'Imagine Mr Carnegie being called a robber and octopus', she said. 'I never heard anything so ridiculous. There wasn't a crooked bone in his body.'

IX

In their maturity, many notable historians have philosophised and theorised about history. There is much ingenuity and sincerity in their disquisitions, but little of practical value, particularly to library historians, most of whom are 'casuals', here today and gone tomorrow.

If all history is of value, then library history is of value; if not, then not. At this point I am bound to quote from A J P Taylor, the well-known British historian, who has done most to stimulate interest in history and said most to belittle its importance. In the *New statesman* Febuary 24th 1978 he wrote: 'In my humble field I stick to my old view that history provides no practical guidance to the problems of the present. History enables us to understand the past better— no more and no less.' Earlier, in the *Observer* October 28th

1969, he asked, 'Why has history, alone among the arts, to be justified by its practical purpose?'

This latter observation was made in the course of a review of J H Plumb's *The death of the past* (Macmillan, 1969), in which Dr Plumb said something about history which those library historians who have by-passed all the theories and philosophies of history will find re-assuring: 'Although historians spend assiduous lives in its practice and perhaps write more than they should about its nature and methods, few in the West are agreed about its purpose or its validity.'

In the larger concerns of national governments, the lessons of history may not be relied upon. When I was young, we did not expect 'The Great War' would become 'World War I'. In more intimate matters, a knowledge of what has gone before is more likely to be of benefit. In librarianship, as in other professions, one needs some knowledge of 'the story so far' to get one's bearings. A recruit to the British public library service who reads Thomas Kelly's *History of public libraries in Great Britain 1845-1975*, if only its final chapter, should be all the better for it. (The final chapter, called 'A decade of change', covers local government re-organisation, the formation of the British Library, the increased attention to 'outreach activities', and the eruption of the public lending right controversy.)

Searching my mind for an instance of undoubted help from historical knowledge in the sphere of librarianship, I recalled Fremont Rider's *The scholar and the future of the research library: a problem and its solution* (New York: Hadham Press, 1944). In this fascinating volume, which I remember reading at one sitting, Rider demonstrated, by statistics, that the great research libraries of the USA were doubling their size every sixteen years, and had been doing so for some time. The appreciation of this historical fact led Rider to consider how these libraries might cope with the accommodation problems presented by this high rate of growth of their stocks. Out of his deliberations came the Microcard.

But perhaps the best way to defend library history is to borrow from a distinguished national historian a passage from his spirited defence of history at large. In his brilliant treatise *The practice of history* (Sydney University Press, 1967;

25

Collins Fontana Library, 1969) G R Elton said: 'It would
certainly be untrue to suppose that history can teach no
practical lessons. It enlarges the area of individual experience by teaching about human behaviour, about man in
relationship to other men. . .' (p 67)

X

What remains to be done in library history will emerge from
the chapters which follow, but there is one matter of such
importance that reference to it should not be delayed. The
greatest problem, and the greatest challenge, in library
history arise from its greatest defect: it is closed circuit
history. If it is not by librarians for librarians, it is by historians for librarians.

A survey of the small number of articles on library history
published in non-library periodicals shows that, apart from
the occasional contributions on libraries which are major
national or regional institutions, what one usually gets is an
illustrated article on some local library which is old enough
to be regarded as quaint—a venerable cathedral library; a
parochial library; a surviving eighteenth-century subscription
library; or a nineteenth-century Scottish miners' library. It
is a well-known fact that there are old libraries in Britain
whose interest to the public depends largely upon the circumstance that the medieval chains which, at some time, had
been removed, have in recent years been restored. (The
chained libraries at Hereford Cathedral and Grantham Parish
Church are good examples.)

The little attention which is paid to libraries in the majority
of social histories of Great Britain may be explained and
defended by the absence, until the recent publications of
Thomas Kelly, of authoritative and wide-ranging histories of
British libraries from which the social historians could draw
either information or references to primary sources.

The need for better representation of libraries in social
histories could be demonstrated at length. They are not
entirely ignored. They have a decent place, as one would
expect, in Asa Briggs' *Victorian cities* (Odhams, 1963);
but rather more typical is the perfunctory reference to them
in Noreen Branson and Margot Heinemann *Britain in the*

nineteen thirties (Weidenfeld & Nicolson, 1971). The Left Book Club is given three pages, the paperback revolution (Penguins) one paragraph, and libraries at large one sentence: 'Books, in the early thirties, were usually borrowed rather than bought—from public libraries, or from Boots, Mudies or other [sic] "twopenny libraries" occupying a few shelves in local shops' (p 278). Although the British public library service was sadly under-developed in the 1930's, I am prepared to argue that it was not all that less important than the Left Book Club.

The most resolute attempt, so far, to take library history into the market place is the lavishly illustrated quarto *Books for the people: an illustrated history of the British public library*, by Thomas Kelly, who provided a readable abstract of his two standard textbooks, and Edith Kelly, who selected the illustrations (Deutsch, 1977). It is too early, yet, to say how successful this experiment may be, but the reviewers, including myself, were more kindly disposed towards the second edition of Professor Kelly's *History of public libraries in Great Britain 1845-1975*, which was published about the same time. Thus, Richard Hoggart, in the *Times literary supplement* December 30th 1977, having commended the major work, saying that it will not easily be replaced, said: 'The other [*Books for the people*] is essentially a large picture book with a fairly skeletal text, drawn from the main history.' Prophecy is easy when one has little to lose by it, but I feel certain that, henceforth, and thanks largely to Professor Kelly, ignorance about our library heritage outside the library profession will diminish, if only slightly.

This, then, is how we stand, in general terms, in the realm of library history. In taking a closer look, in the following chapters, I have considered separately the aspects of time, place, library activity, the history of the individual library, and the biographical approach to library history.

TWO

TIME, PLACE, TYPE OF LIBRARY
AND TYPE OF ACTIVITY

I REMEMBER, as a small boy, sitting in my mother's kitchen gravely regarding a tin of Vim, on which there was a picture of a man holding a tin of Vim, on which (notionally) there was a man.... and so on. A young Einstein would have snared this phenomenon and reduced it, in a trice, to a neat formula. I found it more agreeable to switch my thoughts to something less disturbing.

An even more staggering view of infinity materialises if one estimates all the literature which could conceivably be written on the entire span of history. By about the end of the century an estimate of all that might be written on the history of libraries, merely, will probably paralyse the mind. It does not do so now for several reasons: until the eighteenth century libraries were comparatively few; until the nineteenth century most libraries were impermanent; and, overall, too little pains have been taken to preserve library records.

Nevertheless, there is more than enough literature on library history to tease the bibliographers, exercise the researchers, and confuse the students.

II

Looking for a way to break down the entire literature of library history for examination, the most useful is to divide it according to its main facets: type of library, type of library activity, time, and place.

Taking these in reverse order, and beginning with place: it is evident that most library historians are insular. Many are parochial. There are a few exceptions and most of them are American. They include James Westfall Thompson, authority

29

on the mediaeval library history of Europe; Paul Kaufman, who has diligently explored the history of the community libraries of Britain during the eighteenth century; Barbara McCrimmon, who has made a close study of the Library of the British Museum during the nineteenth century; and Guinevere L Griest, who has done almost all that can be done, in the absence of its archives (a casualty of the World War II blitz, I believe) to revivify that great Victorian institution Mudie's Select Library.(1) British library historians have been less adventurous, in recent years, with the notable exception of Dr K W Humphreys, whose work on the book provisions of the mediaeval friars deserves to be better known.(2)

The boldest library historians are those who have attempted to write a library history either of the world, or of the western world. Few have done so, and none with complete success. There are three arguable reasons for this. One is the lack of national and other large-scale histories, so that the literature which the universal library historian has to grapple with is fragmented to a frightening degree. The second is that although this scattered literature is immense, it still does not cover everything; there are noticeable gaps in our knowledge. 'From a practical point of view. . .it is only in quite recent times that we have acquired an adequate foundation of factual knowledge, and even now for many periods that knowledge has stultifying gaps.' This observation, by Geoffrey Barraclough, was not made about library history, but about general world history; nevertheless, it is as true of the one as it is of the other. This brings us to the third point. 'World history', said Barraclough, 'is not and never can be, the sum or aggregate of national histories.'

Barraclough's recipe for a successful world history is to sacrifice most of the detail in the national histories and concentrate on the general movements and cross-currents which can be handled successfully and which do give history a new dimension. The essay from which these observations are taken is so carefully reasoned that it is worth reading in full. It is called 'Universal history' and it is to be found in *Approaches to history: a symposium* edited by H P R Finberg (Routledge & Kegan Paul, 1962). It explains in part, at least,

30

why works such as Elmer D Johnson and Michael H Harris *History of libraries in the western world* (3rd revised edition, Metchuen NJ, Scarecrow Press, 1976) and Sidney L Jackson *Libraries and librarianship in the west: a brief history* (New York: McGraw-Hill, 1974) are not completely satisfactory. (There are other reasons, including inadequate documentation.)

A library historian who wishes to operate beyond the walls of his own library, or the boundaries of his own city, should take note of what has been done by Ray E Held towards his projected trilogy on the history of the public (or community, as Kaufman would say) libraries of California over the past century. The first volume, *Public libraries in California, 1849-1878* (Berkeley: University of California Press, 1963) was mainly concerned with the social library; the second, *The rise of the public library in California* (Chicago: American Library Association, 1973) began the history of the public library proper, with the promise of a third volume to continue the story. Here is an excellent example of how a library historian may fare when he gives due consideration to the allied but conflicting claims of time, place and type of library.

III

It must be admitted, however, that among the many tasks which library historians may undertake, if they choose, few are more worthy, or potentially more absorbing, than writing the library history of a single town. For a large city, such as Manchester or Chicago, a comprehensive history would be, for most library historians, a challenge too big to accept. What is now abundantly clear is that the library history of even a small town may provide ample scope and interest. Three pertinent examples may be found in Library Association Fellowship theses: R Wilson *A history of King's Lynn libraries 1797-1905* (1971), John Morley *Libraries of Newark-on Trent 1698-1960* (1969) and V J Kite *Libraries in Bath 1618-1964* (1966).

It is quite extraordinary how much of unique interest has come to light through excursions into local library history such as these. The nineteenth century, in particular, only partly covered by Professor Thomas Kelly in his *Early public libraries*, is proving to be an extremely profitable period for research, as it is in many areas of local history. Thus, in recent years, research into urban library history has shown that in Barnsley a long-lived and moderately successful library was operated by the local co-operative society for its members; at Newark an unusually successful book-club existed from 1777 to 1872; at Leicester there were, for some years, two rival private subscriptions libraries; and at King's Lynn, a public subscription library (the Stanley Library) was subsidised by a local philanthropist to deter the local council from levying a library rate.

The advantages of investigating the general library history of a town are multiple: it encourages the historian, far more than the history of a single library would, to take note of the changes in the town's size and character; its wealth, class-structure and cultural and social activities; and it obliges the historian to shift his viewpoint, and, therefore, to make comparisons and contrasts. In short, there is a greater chance, in this kind of endeavour, that the result of a library historian's work will be a genuine contribution to local history, as well as to library history.

Bearing in mind that the majority of libraries are, and have been, local libraries, the place of libraries in the literature of local history is unobtrusive, to say the least. From time to time, librarians with a personal interest in local history have taken it upon themselves to write the history of their own towns. (Examples which come to mind are W C Berwick Sayers on Croydon, Duncan Gray on Nottingham and Mary Walton on Sheffield.) I have yet to come across an example where a librarian local historian has given his section on library history undue prominence. Sometimes, one feels, it has not been given enough.

Overall, libraries have fared badly in the expanding literature on local history, and for this librarians can only blame themselves. I have noticed in some histories of individual towns, and also in some of the more recent manuals on local studies, such as Alan Rogers *This was their world: approaches to local history* (British Broadcasting Corporation, 1972) and Blake McKelvey *The city in American history* (Allen &

32

Unwin, 1969; New York: Barnes & Noble, 1969), fleeting recognition of the fact that libraries have existed and were important in the cultural and educational life of the community, but obvious ignorance of what has been written about them. Even when we have done useful work on our own history, it has not travelled very far.

IV

When G K Chesterton published his *Short history of England*, the public applauded his wit and the scholars questioned his wisdom. But, as always, there was some sense in his verbal frolics. In his introduction, Chesterton referred to an article on English history, in a popular encyclopaedia, which depicted Stephen of Blois 'with one of those helmets with steel brims curved like a crescent, which went with the age of ruffs and trunk hose'. 'Helmets', said Chesterton, 'were medieval, and any old helmet was good enough for Stephen.'(3)

Although carelessness of this kind is less common today, a basic truth remains. For reasons which may have their roots in temperament, as much as in education, those who care for history are likely to prefer one of its broad eras— ancient, medieval or modern—more than the others. This is commonplace and also inevitable; but in the wake of preference comes knowledge, and in the wake of rejection, ignorance.

In his article 'Ancient and medieval libraries' in the *Encyclopedia of library and information science*, Raymond Irwin said, 'The early history of libraries is in part a matter of guesswork.' Certainly, the library historian who chooses to labour in the ancient period requires not only an intimate knowledge of the ancient civilisations, but the ability to stimulate interest in the bibliothecal aspects of them, on which our knowledge is scanty. It was a particular merit of Irwin himself that he was able to do this, for the libraries of ancient Greece and Rome, among those who could neither identify Lucius Annaeus Seneca, nor locate Alexandria on the map. Irwin's literary skill was such that one scarcely realises the limitations of the materials at his disposal.

If one begins the study of ancient library history by reading Sir Frederic Kenyon's short article 'Libraries' in the

Oxford classical dictionary, or, for that matter, the ancient history section of Irwin's article in the *Encyclopedia of library and information science*, what Irwin contrived to do with the story of ancient libraries in his companion volumes of essays on library history, *The heritage of the English library* (Allen & Unwin, 1964) and *The English library: sources and history* (Allen & Unwin, 1966) comes as a surprise. In the latter volume there is a chapter called 'In Roman Britain' which begins, disarmingly, with the observation:

'I suppose that the average historian of libraries would omit any chapter on the libraries of Roman Britain, for there is no direct evidence that any existed. That is not the whole of the story, however, as I hope to show.'(4)

I have said elsewhere that ancient library history is like a jigsaw from which most of the pieces are missing. Medieval library history is not much better.

Professor Kelly, who was trained as a medieval historian, has said that, when turning to modern history, he felt there was a superfluity of records. A familiar example of inadequate information in the medieval period is the story of the libraries of the English religious houses. The destruction of catalogues, furniture, and library rooms, where they existed, as well as of books, has left us with only fragmentary information on most of these collections, which for their day were often unusually large. Occasionally the Department of the Environment is able to put a metal plaque, with the legend LIBRARY, against a shattered wall, or the speculative legend LIBRARY CUPBOARD against an empty recess; but there are instances, as at Leicester, where although we know from surviving documents that there was special accommodation for books, nothing at all can be seen now. Professor David Knowles, who was not himself an expert on monastic libraries, but who skilfully summarised the writings on them by M R James and others in his classic works *The monastic order in England* (Cambridge University Press, 1940) 522-527 and *The religious orders in England* vol II (Cambridge University Press, 1955) 331-353, said that he thought that, all extant documents on them having been examined, the time had come for a general 'synthetic history' of the mediaeval monastic libraries.(5)

Ernest A Savage was neither an academic nor a mediaevalist, but a public librarian with an abiding interest in library history and enough confidence and energy to accomplish anything he had a mind to do. His major contribution to library history, *Old English libraries: the making, collection and use of books during the Middle Ages* (Methuen, 1911) is a competent piece of work, still in print.(6) But what Savage should have given us was a history of the public library movement in Great Britain. What might have come from that exercise one may shrewdly guess from his long, characteristically didactic review of W A Munford's *Penny rate* (Library Association, 1951), *Library Association record* 53 (9) September 1951, 303-305.

There are some reviews which, because of the facts they add, or the opinions they offer, are so much worth reading in conjunction with the books they assess, that it would be a boon and a delight to readers if they could be incorporated in any reprints of them which may be called for. Savage's review of *Penny rate* is a prime example. If this suggestion seems fanciful, I would point out that when *The medieval library* by James Westfall Thompson (University of Chicago Press, 1939) was reprinted (New York: Hafner, 1957), it included, as an appendix, the meticulous review of it by Blanche B Boyer which had appeared in the *Library quarterly*.

It is a pity Savage did not live long enough to read Professor Kelly's great history of the British public library. As Savage was a constructive, and not merely a caustic, critic, we have probably lost a review of Kelly's *History of public libraries in Great Britain* which Professor Kelly himself might have relished.

V

It was as much for his own benefit, as for ours, that Professor Kelly paved the way for his *History of public libraries in Great Britain* by tracing the history of the various endowed libraries and subscription libraries (referred to collectively by Paul Kaufman as 'community libraries') which had been provided for the public before the inauguration of the rate-supported public library service. The result was the familiar, perennially useful *Early public libraries: a history of public libraries in Great Britain before 1850* (Library Association, 1966).

But when Professor Kelly set about writing *Early public libraries*, he was faced with a problem which, surprisingly, previous library historians had ignored: the classification and nomenclature of libraries. What came of his deliberations on this subject may be found in *Early public libraries* Appendix I 'Library nomenclature'. No student of library history should fail to read this, or any researcher, either. One may not agree with it (a classification scheme must always reflect the predilections and viewpoint of its maker) but one can hardly deny that some kind of classification is necessary, if only because, over the years, the names of libraries have been used very loosely. For example, the famous Leeds Library (founded 1768), a proprietary, or private subscription library, has in its day been called a public library and a circulating library.(7)

The main classes of Professor Kelly's scheme are public libraries, endowed libraries, subscription libraries and institutional libraries, the basis of the classification being ownership. The last group, institutional libraries, is the broadest, as it covers a wide variety of libraries: university and college, church and cathedral, learned society, professional association, government, industrial and many others. (Turning to the USA, one discovers, without much surprise, several terms not in use in Great Britain, eg, social libraries and mercantile libraries.)

One day we will have general histories of each major type of library, but progress is bound to be slow, owing to the lack of histories of individual libraries. Two particularly awkward cases are the histories of the libraries of the mechanics' institutes and the commercial circulating (rental) libraries, for the simple reason that almost all of them, whether large or small, have disappeared—many of them long since, leaving behind no more than an entry in a local directory, or, if one is lucky, a printed catalogue. For the private subscription (proprietary, or social) libraries the chance of writing a general history are somewhat better, as several notable examples still survive, or survived until recently, and their records are available. In Britain, happily, we still have the great London Library, the Leeds Library, the Portico Library, Manchester, the Bromley House Library, Nottingham, and the Penzance Library.

VI
To the students of library history, the lack of general histories, especially national histories and histories of the major types of libraries, is a grave disadvantage, as courses in library history are usually short and students, therefore, have little time in which to acquire, read and digest the miscellany of articles, pamphlets, chapters in books, and so forth, which are the only sources of information on a number of topics. A broad syllabus is all very well, providing the students are at liberty to move at will within it, concentrating on those areas where they feel they can learn and discover most effectively; but the examination system too often encourages skimming and a desperate reliance on lecture notes, so that the only benefit of a course in library history may be that it gives the student a glimpse of a wide and enticing territory which he may return to later, and explore at leisure.

Now that we have Professor Kelly's *History of public libraries in Great Britain*, the lack of comparable histories on other types of libraries is more obvious and more keenly felt. At this point, however, it is appropriate to pay tribute to what I call the reconnoitring library historians—those who have had the courage to make a tentative, pioneering survey of a broad area of library history and have dared to publish their findings, knowing that there is much still to be done, and that later explorers may well upset their facts and conclusions. A splendid example is Frank Beckwith 'The eighteenth-century proprietary library in England' *Journal of documentation* 3 (2) September 1947, 81-98. It was this pioneering survey, I believe, which led Paul Kaufman to explore the history of the forgotten eighteenth century book clubs. The result was another valuable reconnoitring report, 'English book clubs and their role in social history' *Libri* 14 (1) 1964, 1-31.

The history of our modern university libraries, which is at last receiving deserved attention, was first explored by E G

Baxter in 'A preliminary historical survey of developments in university libraries in Great Britain 1919-1950' *Library Association record* 56 (9-10) September-October 1954, 330-335, 389-393. This has now been augmented by Norman Roberts 'Aspects of British university librarianship' *College and research libraries* 38 (6) November 1977, 460-476. In the USA, the modern history of academic libraries has been the subject of a team reconnaissance: *Libraries for teaching: libraries for research; essays for a century* edited by Richard D Johnson (Chicago: American Library Association, 1977), written in honour of the ALA's centennial.

An area of library history which, until recently, seemed to have no appeal at all to library historians was the history of the industrial special library; but here, also, we have a reconnaissance report, namely a Library Association Fellowship thesis (1968) by Margaret R Marshall, which she summarised in 'British industrial libraries before 1939' *Journal of documentation* 28 (2) June 1972, 107-121.

VII

One of the characteristics of the histories of institutions is that more is likely to be known about their beginnings than their ends. Beginnings are exciting and full of promise, sometimes attended with elaborate ceremonial, or still better recalled because they were the culmination of a long period of struggle. Endings are likely to be less memorable, especially if they are the quiet termination of a long period of steady decline, so that, at the end, there are few assets to realise, few members to turn away. This was often the fate of the mechanics' institutes and their libraries. In its early days, everything to do with the movement was news. There were several national surveys of the institutes, but none after 1851. This, as Professor Kelly explains, is a hindrance to historians, as:

'Except for the handful of institutions which have been fortunate enough to find a historian, we must rely on such odd scraps of information as can be picked up from local histories and guide-books, reports of unions [of mechanics' institutes], where they existed, reports of the Society of Arts, and occasional references in memoirs and biographies of the period.'(8)

By contrast, the lack of general studies of the history of the English cathedral libraries is less likely to be due to lack of sources of information, which are fairly plentiful, than to the scattering of them through many books, pamphlets and periodicals, to say nothing of manuscripts. But thanks to the efforts of E Anne Read, all these materials have been brought under control in *A checklist of books, catalogues and periodical articles relating to the cathedral libraries of England* (Oxford Bibliographical Society, Occasional Publications no 6, 1970) a pioneering work which she had now corrected and extended, so that it now covers the libraries of the modern cathedrals, such as Birmingham, Liverpool and Truro, in 'Cathedral libraries: a supplementary checklist' *Library history* 4 (5) Spring 1978, 141-163.

VIII

Although it is evident from the pages of *Library history* that library historians are quite eager to explore the histories of parochial libraries, subscription libraries, circulating libraries and university libraries, when it comes to writing a major work on library history the rate-supported public library has a very strong pull. This needs little explanation; it certainly needs little justification. Public libraries are numerous. They are also, despite changes in local government organisation, permanent. Although they have not taken enough care of their archives, archives are there, in plenty. But the proliferation of records is probably not the only reason why public library history is popular with library historians.

There was endless debate as to whether public libraries should be established. How this debate was conducted, nationally and locally, has already given several library historians a challenging opportunity to prove their mettle. Public libraries have had enemies as vigorous as their supporters. They have also been served by some of the most dedicated and inventive librarians the profession has known.

Thomas Kelly's work on the history of the British public library has been outstanding, but it is not isolated. It was preceded by W J Murison *The public library: its origins, purpose, and significance* (Harrap, first published 1955, 2nd revised edition, 1971), which deals in some detail with

39

the development of public library purpose in Britain, and by W R Aitken *History of the public library movement in Scotland* (Glasgow: Scottish Library Association, 1971), the most outstanding contribution to the library history of a nation which has made several peculiarly interesting contributions to library progress; and recently it has been followed by John E Pemberton *Politics and public libraries in England and Wales 1850-1970* (Library Association, 1977) which traces the growth of the pressures for reform of the public library service which eventually brought about the liberal Public Libraries and Museums Act 1964, and by R J B Morris *Parliament and the public libraries: a survey of legislative activity promoting the municipal library service in England and Wales, 1850-1976* (Mansell, 1977), a massive work of meticulous scholarship by a sympathetic 'outsider'. (Mr Morris is Associate Town Clerk of Grimsby.)

With such works as these, there is no shred of justification for either ignoring, or despising, the public library when tracing the social history of modern Britain.

The books by Aitken, Pemberton and Morris are all texts of theses. In this they are typical of much of the solid work which is now being done on library history on both sides of the Atlantic. They also point to the likely future of library history in Great Britain in another respect: the strengthening of public library history by concentrating on a period, aspect, or regional study of it. It is, I think, a very promising outlook.

IX

When library historians have a mind to deal with some aspect of librarianship, some type of library activity, there is no telling where they will end up. There are some obvious choices: library classification, cataloguing, reference work, work with young people, for example; all of which, in fact, have been tackled with varying degrees of success. There are also some quite unexpected choices, such as D W Davies *Public libraries as culture and social centers: the origin of the concept* (Metuchen NJ: Scarecrow Press, 1974) an amusing, if not very profound study of the development of extension activities ('fiestas, festivals and exhibitions' and so forth) in

American and British libraries; and Harry R Skallerup *Books afloat and ashore: a history of books, libraries and reading among seamen during the age of sail* (Hamden, Conn: Shoestring Press, 1974).

A pioneer of offbeat library histories, and an outstanding one at that, was R C Barrington Partridge *The history of legal deposit of books throughout the British Empire* (Library Association, 1938). Written when library history in Britain was remarkable neither for its quantity nor its quality, Partridge's book took as its subject a topic whose very name meant little to most librarians and dealt with it thoroughly; but without, by any means, extinguishing its abiding interest as a source of controversy.

Since the war, the major British achievements in tracing the history of specific library activities have been of rather wider appeal. George Jefferson *Library co-operation* (2nd edition, Deutsch, 1977) is not wholly historical, but because library co-operation in Great Britain has twisted roots, by which I mean that it has grown rather oddly, and in several directions at once, Dr Jefferson has wisely given his treatise a sound historical foundation. Here is a very good example of how useful historical knowledge can be in gaining a proper understanding of current library practice.

Alec Ellis, in his *Library services for young people in England and Wales 1830-1970* (Oxford: Pergamon Press, 1971) is not quite so successful in bringing his subject to life. It was when reviewing this book that Enid M Osborne said that 'the historical approach to any subject often conflicts with readability', but it was a subject well worth tackling, and it has been admirably researched and scrupulously documented.

X

As librarianship becomes more complex, as new services and new techniques come into being, the boundaries of library history, already extremely wide, will become wider still. We shall, therefore, have new topics to deal with when we are still flirting with old ones. Prominent among these is library architecture. It has not altogether been ignored, but most of what has been written about it has been written incidentally, in histories of architecture and comprehensive studies of the work of individual architects. Over the last decade a little work has been done specifically on the history of library architecture. In the first volume of *British library history: bibliography* there was no heading for library architecture; in the second, which covers the years 1969-1972 there is.

Two interesting examples of what may be done with this absorbing topic, even on a small scale, are Denis F Keeling 'British public library buildings 1850-1870' *Library history* 1 (4) Autumn 1968, 100-126 (which I could have cited earlier as an example of what I have called reconnoitring studies) and Michael Dewe 'H T Hare: Edwardian library architect' *Library review* vol 26 Summer 1978, 80-84.

Mr Dewe concludes his article by saying: 'The history of library buildings has been neglected in this country and the United States.' This is fair comment. One interesting contribution to the subject in the USA is Donald E Oehlerts 'Sources for the study of American library architecture' *Journal of library history* 11(1) January 1976, 68-78, which shows that although useful sources of information exist, they are widely scattered.

The problem in this field of study is that the library historian needs not only a knowledge of libraries but of architecture, and the ability to appreciate both architects' and librarians' problems. It will be a great boon when more library historians have the confidence to tackle the history of library architecture, as the architectural historians are liable to praise a library for its aesthetic virtues and leave practical considerations on one side.

Alastair Service, in his *Edwardian architecture: a handbook to building design in Britain 1890-1914* (Thames & Hudson, 1977) mentions favourably public library buildings at Edinburgh, Bristol, Wolverhampton and Lincoln, the John Rylands Library, Manchester ('Champneys achieved brilliant spatial effects in the interior') and, inevitably, the library wing of the Glasgow School of Art by Charles Rennie Mackintosh ('the finest interior of all the great Scottish architect's work'). It would be interesting to know how successful these buildings were, from the point of view of staff and readers, when they were new. They are probably

42

inadequate in many ways now. I remember asking a chief librarian if it was true that one of his branch libraries was a 'listed' building, meaning was it legally protected against destruction and major alteration. He swore and said that it was.

A dossier of extraordinary interest could be built up by anyone with access to files of back issues of architectural periodicals and a photocopier. Among the plans of libraries which could be copied there are some of libraries which were designed but never built, among them the original St Pancras central library.

XI
Finally, library history must encompass the histories of the library associations and the major periodicals of librarianship. Here, Britain is ahead of the USA. Neither the American Library Association (founded 1876) nor the Library Association (founded 1877) failed to mark its centennial with becoming festivities, but the LA did so with a large-scale published history, W A Munford *History of the Library Association 1877-1977* (Library Association, 1976); the ALA did not, although it has superior archives.(9)

Writing the history of a library association must be the most difficult library history assignment of all. I cannot answer for the ALA, but I know that, in the conduct of the LA's affairs, there was, for some years, a 'wrangle of disinclination' (to borrow a phrase from Stephen Leacock) between several of its leading councillors. How much of this will eventually be recorded remains to be seen. In the meantime we have a welcome history of the LA which shows that it was never idle and seldom foolish, but for too many years, like the profession it served, sadly 'disadvantaged'.

No young library historian's heart is likely to beat any the faster at being told that there is work to be done on the history of the major periodicals of librarianship; but the long established mainstream periodicals, such as the *Library journal*, the *Library Association record* and the *Library world*, each has a story of hazards, failures and successes which, for sheer interest, can match anything else in library history. This is because these general periodicals are the

43

forums of the profession; and being so, they themselves can provoke criticism for allowing too little, or too much freedom of expression. The only library periodical whose history has been written with the frankness and zest it deserves is the *Library world* (now the *New library world*), founded by James Duff Brown to guide the profession with an independent light, which it still does. When it reached its 800th issue, in February 1967, it celebrated the occasion with a sprightly symposium by K C Harrison (its then editor), W A Munford and Clive Bingley. K C Harrison also wrote the excellent article 'Library World (New Library World)' for the *Encyclopedia of library and information science*. It is a pity that the brief article on the *Library journal* does not match it.

THREE

THE INDIVIDUAL LIBRARY

THE NUMBER of histories of individual libraries which have been written is a good deal less than the number of libraries which have existed. Nevertheless, if we take into account the many small-scale histories which have been written (pamphlets, chapters in books, articles in periodicals and newspapers) the total is much larger than is generally realised. In recent years its growth has been stimulated by the publication of histories designed to honour centenaries and jubilees, and the choice of individual libraries as the subjects of theses on library history, in preference to topics embracing many libraries.

An obvious question to ask is 'Does every library deserve a history?' In my view, it does. Providing the materials are available (a condition which rules out, unfortunately, thousands of libraries which no longer exist) and a proper sense of proportion is observed, every library should have its history. Why not? We do not jib at the idea of every church, chapel, school, or place of entertainment having its history. The justification for writing the histories of individual libraries is no less. Apart from their significance in the lives of the communities to which they belonged, each library will have had its own identity. Even where there has been similarity in age, resources and activities, the differences in environment and staff will have engendered features of unique interest. This point came to be well appreciated by Thomas Kelly as he accumulated information for his comprehensive *History of public libraries in Great Britain 1845-1975*. 'The heart of library history', he said, 'is not to be found in its more general aspects, such as the growth of library legislation, or the development of library techniques, important as these things are. Rather it is to be sought in the often highly individual history of the hundreds of individual libraries which together make up the library service.'(1)

The task of writing general histories of libraries, such as Professor Kelly's, is not literally impossible, but scarcely worthwhile without the histories of individual libraries to draw upon. On the other hand, such are the variations in the histories of individual libraries, that the more the general historian has to take into account, the more difficult his task becomes.

However, the present position is that a great deal of work still needs to be done on the history of individual libraries. Many histories which could be written, as the materials are available, have yet to be attempted; and some which have been written are inadequate and will have to be replaced.

No one knows, precisely, what libraries have existed. But thanks to the diligence of Thomas Kelly, who has gathered together details of hundreds of what he calls 'endowed libraries' founded between the Reformation and 1800, and the complementary labours of the American scholar Paul Kaufman, who has compiled tentative lists of the circulating and subscription libraries which existed before 1800, we now know the names, at least, of many British libraries whose existence had either been forgotten, or had never been known outside their own localities.(2) The tally is incomplete for the years up to 1800 and one must add to it, of course, a host of libraries, many defunct, which appeared in the nineteenth century—the libraries of the Sunday schools, mechanics' institutes, learned societies, professional associations, subscription libraries, circulating libraries, the libraries of government departments, private firms, schools, colleges and universities, to say nothing of the rate-supported public libraries. The compilation of a comprehensive list of British libraries established since 1800 is a gargantuan task which no one is anxious to attempt.

II

The history of many libraries of the past is a cipher and will remain so. Regrettably, this observation applies to some libraries which existed within living memory. When they disappeared, their archives disappeared with them.

46

Where a library still exists, it might be supposed that the historian's overriding difficulty would be that of selecting and organising facts, as distinct from tediously searching for them. In reality, the discovery of facts may still be difficult, even impossible. One of the stated objects of the Library Association Library History Group is to 'foster the preservation of records of library development'. What the Group might do, effectively, in pursuit of this object, I am not sure; but I hope that, one day, it will pay some attention to it.

Generally speaking, a large library is more likely to take care of its own archives than a small one, although perhaps I should say 'preserve' rather than 'take care', as there is a difference between keeping records in existence, on the one hand, and caring for them, so that they are organised for instant use, on the other.

The kinds of records a library may have on its own history will depend, to some extent, on the kind of library it is, more particularly upon whether it is public or non-public. But the documents one usually hopes to find are reports (serial and *ad hoc*) minutes of the meetings of the governing body, statistics, architectural plans, photographs (and, for a very old library, prints), clippings of references to the library in newspapers and periodicals and (if optimism runs really high) selected correspondence.

Human nature being what it is, it is perhaps inevitable that librarians should be more enthusiastic about collecting, preserving and indexing documents on any local, or national, institution other than their own. No one type of library, I believe, is more negligent in this respect than any other, and I draw my examples from public libraries because it is mainly in the public library sector that my own researches in library history have been done.

As most public libraries have special collections on local history, it never ceases to amaze me that a library which can produce, on demand, cascades of information on the history of the Town Hall, the grammar school, the Unitarian chapel in the High Street and the dismantled bicycle factory in Eastgate, should have the greatest difficulty in providing anything at all on its own history.

I remember visiting a large city library which had recently passed, but not blithely celebrated, its hundredth birthday.

My hopeful request for information on its history was met with puzzlement, back-stage whispers among the reference staff, and the eventual production of a skimpy article published in the 1880's. Under pressure, the staff later produced a file of printed annual reports—incomplete, I need hardly say. I was offered no newscuttings. They had none to offer. At another central public library I did find newscuttings, but with massive gaps. In a third public library, again the central library of a large city, my request for illustrations of the interior of the former central library (occupied for nearly seventy years) produced one photograph, taken by the local press, of the lending library in the 1930's. I felt pretty certain that, in this carefully posed and quite unnatural picture, several of the 'readers' were members of the staff.

At another central library of a large borough I was quite confident that I would find a substantial archive on the period I was interested in, as it was then that the library achieved renown as a pacemaker in public library development, under the energetic leadership of a chief librarian whose name is still familiar. But I was wrong. The local history librarian explained, apologetically, that a later incumbent had had a thorough 'clear-out'. At the splendid little public library of one of our older towns I found a very good collection of records, including a correspondence book which had carbons of letters which the Edwardian librarian had sent to several of the leaders of the profession, including James Duff Brown, seeking their advice. But their replies had not been preserved.

To be fair, a library is not always to blame for the gaps in its own archives. Fires, floods and bombings have taken their toll, and what kind of minutes were kept of the library committee, or board of trustees, may have been beyond the library's jurisdiction. I remember my surprise when, having spent many hours in other public libraries grappling with council minutes which concealed more than they revealed, I came upon the printed minutes of the former London Borough of St Pancras for the early years of the century. In the compilation of these marvellously revealing records, it would seem that St Pancras had enjoyed the help of St Peter. There was irony in this, as when these minutes were compiled, the Borough Council was hell-bent on closing down its only library. (It could not legally do this, but it could, and did, refuse to add to this solitary branch the three other branches and a central library which had been approved by an earlier Council.)

Probably no library historian has been wholly satisfied with his materials; but, in my experience, exasperation reaches its peak when one discovers that, although the required information exists, it has to be painfully disinterred. An all too familiar example is scanning the fragile, or microfilmed pages of unindexed newspapers—a gruelling task which should be offered in prisons as a reasonable alternative to picking oakum.

III

Few large-scale histories of individual libraries are published histories. This is not entirely due to economic reasons. It is true that the publication of the history of an individual library is unlikely to be a profitable venture, but there are some libraries whose eminence, prestige and wide readership are enough to ensure that their published histories would, at least, break even. I have in mind, particularly, those libraries which, in function, if not in name, are national libraries. In Britain, this definition encompasses the former British Museum Library (now a major part of the British Library Reference Division), the London Library and the Bodleian Library, Oxford; three remarkable institutions which command from their readers more than token respect. Detailed, comprehensive histories do not exist for any of them.

For the British Museum Library there is an authoritative, well-written history by the late Arundell Esdaile, *The British Museum Library* (Allen & Unwin, 1946), but it is quite a short history and does not cover any of the remarkable changes which have taken place since the war. For the London Library (which had the misfortune to reach its centennial in the bleak year 1941) there is a scattering of admirable articles in periodicals and chapters in books, but no large-scale history. For the Bodleian there is Sir Edmund Craster's *History of the Bodleian Library 1845-1945* (Oxford University Press, 1952), which Arundell Esdaile called 'the

49

most readable and most rewarding book that has been written on library history'. It is certainly very fine, but it covers only one hundred years out of nearly four hundred.

Turning to the USA, we find a situation very similar; for the Library of Congress a readable, authoritative, but small-scale history by David C Mearns, *The story up to now: the Library of Congress 1800-1946* (Washington: Government Printing Office, 1947), which needs up-dating, for Harvard University Library, like the Bodleian Library, a considerable but scattered literature, and for New York Public Library a splendid fragment by Phyllis Dain, *The New York Public Library: a history of its founding and early years* (New York Public Library, 1972), although I believe there is a likelihood of this being augmented.

One is led to the conclusion that the writing of a detailed history of a major library which has existed for some years is a task from which most library historians shrink, not surprisingly, as it not only calls for ample time, financial support, and enormous resolution, but ready and continuous access to the library's records. This means, that it is seldom a feasible task for an 'outsider'. Turning back to the histories of great libraries mentioned above, one finds that most of them were written by 'insiders'. Thus, Arundell Esdaile was Secretary to the Trustees of the British Museum, Sir Edmund Craster was one of Bodley's librarians, and David C Mearns was Director of the Reference Department of the Library of Congress.

Writing the history of a library for which one has oneself had some responsibility is a delicate task, but unless librarians who are qualified to do it can be encouraged to attempt it, the histories of some of our greatest libraries are unlikely to be written.(3)

The major published histories of individual libraries are mostly American, with public libraries well represented. Among the public library histories are several which, in scale, authority and appreciation of the role and influence of public libraries in the community, have no counterpart in the literature of British library history. Outstanding examples are *The Chicago Public Library, origins and backgrounds* by Gwladys Spencer (Chicago: University of Chicago

50

Press, 1943), which is often bracketed with the regional histories of Jesse H Shera and Sidney Ditzion, published during the same decade, as one of the first authentic library histories to be written in the USA; *Boston Public Library: a centennial history* by Walter Muir Whitehill (Cambridge, Mass; Harvard University Press, 1956); and *Open shelves and open minds: a history of the Cleveland Public Library* by C H Cramer (Cleveland: Press of Case Western Reserve University, 1972). To these may be added, although Jesse Shera would dispute it, *Parnassus on Main Street: a history of the Detroit Public Library* by Frank B Woodford (Detroit: Wayne State University Press, 1965). None of these histories, incidentally, was written by a member of the library's own staff.

These histories are exceptional. As Sidney Ditzion complained, the bulk of American public library histories have been written by 'local library employees untrained in the art of asking the past to answer the right and important questions'.

Not one of the British public libraries which has chosen to mark its centennial by the publication of an official history has been either able, or willing, to venture beyond a miniature history, usually a pamphlet. For the large and old established libraries, such as those at Birmingham, Liverpool and Manchester, these pamphlet histories are far too brief for the stories they have to tell. Furthermore, many of them are sadly representative of the traditional, amateurish style of writing local history, rather than the present style, which has its roots in the discipline of the university and polytechnic history departments, especially the developing departments of local studies. Among the few public library histories worthy of mention are the *City Libraries of Sheffield 1856-1956* (Sheffield Libraries, Museums and Art Galleries Committees, 1956), which was written, anonymously, by Miss Mary Walton, the city's contemporary historian, and *City of Norwich Libraries: history and treasures* by Philip Hepworth and Mary Alexander (Norwich: Jarrold & Sons, 1957).

Apart from the lack of historical training, the hazards which have prevented us from having a whole series of public library histories which were valuable contributions to both library and local history are inadequate financial support for the necessary research, and a decent standard of publication, and deficiencies in libraries' archives. I suspect, also, that some libraries are so ashamed of the lean years when they were unable to achieve a proper standard of service that they have little desire to retrace them.

IV

The market for library histories being what it is, most of the large-scale histories of individual libraries written so far would never have been undertaken at all other than as theses. Some of these thesis-histories are very good (a tribute, in part, to their supervisors); and it is, therefore, fortunate that, through the aid of Zerography and microphotography, they should have been given at least a small circulation.

The number of thesis-histories of individual libraries is increasing steadily, mainly for reasons of expediency. Having a mind to work in the field of library history, but lacking the resources to travel in search of information, the thesis writer turns thankfully to the history of the library where he is employed, if it has not already been chronicled.

In his review of *Parnassus on Main Street*, Jesse H Shera said: 'There is nothing unique, or even particularly striking, in this history of Detroit Public Library', and he wondered whether almost 500 pages were necessary to tell it. Proportion in writing the history of a library is important, but the implications of this remark will not be fully appreciated until one has had a good grounding in library history.

A possible situation in Britain would be to find in one particular city (let us take an imaginary one and call it Barset) a cathedral library about 600 years old, a public library seventy years old, and an industrial library only thirty years old. Observing the precept of fair proportion, one might conclude that the history of the public library deserves six times as much space as the history of the cathedral library, and that the history of the cathedral library deserves half as much space as the history of the industrial library. The explanation? Apart form the purging of books which took place during the Tudor period, and the casual destruction which occurred during the Civil War (both thinly documented), the history of the cathedral library has been a story of slow progress interspersed with periods of gentle decay. The only way to produce a substantial history of this library would be to linger over its treasures, describing their history and their features; in other words, to turn the history into a treatise on historical bibliography. This might be worth doing, but it is marginal to library history.

The public library is only of medium size, the population of Barset being about 100,000, but it came into being after a long and bitter feud between rival factions on the City Council, and in the town itself, which delayed adoption of the Public Libraries Acts, and the inauguration of a public library service, for nearly fifty years.(4) Thanks to the industry of the local press, a handsome thesis could be written on this part of the public library's history alone. Add to this that the first librarian was 'a pushing young particle', who eventually became President of the Library Association and a librarian-select in *Who's who*, and that the third librarian was a pioneer in library services to the disadvantaged, and it is clear that the history of the Barset City Libraries is worth lingering over.

The industrial library, which belongs to the research and development department of a firm of international renown, came into being during the immediate post-war period, when the government's stern message to industry was 'Export or starve'. In more ways than one, this library has shown that it believes in the equation 'Good information = Good profits'. It became well-known in its early days for its faceted classification scheme and later for its elaborate series of information bulletins. It may be too early to attempt the history of this library, but if it survives (industrial libraries are likely casualties in recessions and takeovers) a jubilee history should be well worth while.

The history of special libraries, I may add, has been too much neglected. It is true that most of them are still quite young. Most of the special libraries in Great Britain were not established until after World War II. But there are quite a few notable exceptions, among them the libraries of learned societies and professional associations. Their histories may, of course, be taken care of, after a fashion, in the histories of the parent institutions—if they are ever written. But the histories of special libraries present a problem. The records of a public library, perhaps of an academic library, are accessible to all comers. The records of a special library are not. Therefore, interest in library history must be fostered in special libraries, otherwise library history will develop lopsided.

V

Between a large and old established library and a small and fairly new one, say between the Library of Congress and the public library of Wrightsville, or between the Bodleian Library and the Technical College Library at Coketown, there are so many differences in scale that the problems involved in writing the history of the one will inevitably be far greater and far more complex than those involved in writing the history of the other. That much is hardly worth saying. But some of the problems will, in essence, be common to both. The most likely, and also the most regrettable, will be gaps in the records; due not merely to accidental or deliberate destruction, but to the absence of those which would have been helpful if only they had been compiled.

This last point is of some interest and calls for at least one comment. Except in a few instances, the histories of individual libraries are usually based exclusively on the written records, and the written or verbal recollections, of their staffs. The testimony of the readers is seldom in evidence. Even when it is available it is not necessarily of much value; except, perhaps, for its humour. To take an example, imaginary but not far removed from some I have actually encountered: 'The lending librarian was an irritable old man, with a pointed beard and gold-rimmed spectacles, who was always shouting at us kids to keep quiet.'

When library historians have come to terms with the techniques of oral history, the recollections of readers may become a more significant ingredient in the histories of individual libraries. Meantime, we must be content with the small body of published recollections by well-known authors and journalists about the libraries which gladdened their younger days or sustained their professional labours.

A delightful example is to be found in the *Autobiography* of the late Sir Neville Cardus, which vividly recalls his experiences at the Manchester Central Library at the turn of the century; how he drove himself to 'an acute state of myopia' with books borrowed from the lending library, and how, when he had walked out of a job he took refuge from the cold in the reference library. 'The warm air from the bumping pipes already heating, the odour and taste of the rubbermats, the long tables, the rows of books, the gathering traffic of Manchester outside' were the remembered features of his 'Ivory Tower', in which, tentatively, he began to explore 'all schools of thought'. As it turned out, his surreptitious hours spent in the public library were not entirely wasted.(5)

It is not the local public libraries, however, but the great research libraries which have called forth most of the recollections of library users. Two of the great libraries of London are particularly well favoured—the British Museum Library, and what is, to many scholars, its unofficial complement, the London Library in St James's Square. On the former, I recall particularly the drily amusing causerie by 'J Penn' called *For readers only* (Chapman & Hall, 1936) and on the latter the engaging symposium first published in the 400th issue of *Adam*, the international review, in 1977, and later reprinted in book form under the title *The London Library* (Ipswich: Boydell Press, 1978). Happy the library which can earn the declared gratitude of readers such as Lord David Cecil, Angus Wilson, Anthony Powell, Roy Fuller, Edna O'Brien and Colin Wilson.

Among the records which will almost certainly be available for an existing library are statistics. It is almost worth while to condemn oneself to the labour of writing a history of a library to gain a fuller insight into the peculiarities of library statistics.

At this point, I find myself recalling the end of my first day's work in a public library, perched wearily on the edge of a stool in the central lending department 'doing the issue'. This meant dividing the charges, first of all, into fiction and non-fiction, and then sorting the latter into ten piles, one for each of the main classes of the Decimal Classification, counting the piles and entering the results in a ledger. These daily statistics were totalled weekly, monthly and annually, when they were given the cachet of approximate immortality in the library's printed annual report. We had no notion what benefits might be derived from these skeletal statistics, as we were encouraged to accept rather than criticise, to learn by rote rather than ask awkward questions.

Thirty years later, I made some observations on public reference library statistics which broadly indicate what is wrong with many of the statistics which library historians have to cope with:

'The best that can be said of existing reference statistics is that the fluctuations in them are of interest, even though the individual figures do not mean very much. Roughly, reference statistics may be compared with the readings of an uncalibrated thermometer—it cannot register the actual temperature, but it indicates that the temperature rises and falls. But even this is a poor analogy. A reference library which in one month had 6,000 readers and dealt with 1,000 queries may have been busier (in service to the public) some other month when it had 5,000 readers and dealt with 800 queries, for reasons too well known to enumerate.'[6]

In the biennial reports on Edinburgh Public Libraries which Ernest A Savage compiled during the inter-war years, there were no tables of statistics. I have never read any better library reports.

VI

If what I have said so far is correct, it is clear that the situation with regard to the histories of individual libraries is in many ways unsatisfactory, but not altogether for reasons which can be helped. But there is one common defect which could and should be helped, as Thomas Kelly is acutely aware.

During the writing of his *Early public libraries*, and still more in the writing of his *History of public libraries in Great Britain 1845-1975*, Professor Kelly must have read more histories of individual libraries, published and unpublished, than anyone else. Some, especially thesis histories, he found very good; others, especially some of the pamphlet histories, he found very bad:

'The weakness of so many of these histories is that the story of the library is almost completely insulated from every other kind of development, either national or local. We are told about the origins of the library, about its buildings, its benefactors, the development of its services, and so forth, but were it not for the names of people and places it might as well be in Timbuktu for all the attention that is given to the general background.'(7)

The defect of insulation is not, in fact, peculiar to published histories; it is to be found in thesis histories as well, for although background information is seldom entirely absent from a thesis, it is liable to be provided sparingly and grudgingly.

I am talking now about context, a problem more complicated than it may seem at first sight. For one thing, it is not a single but a dual problem. On the one hand there is local context (for an institutional library the history of the institution, for a community library the history of the community); on the other hand there is professional context, how the development of library X compared with, and was influenced by, the development of other libraries of its period.

I do not believe the problem of context is unrecognised. It is more likely that the hard-pressed library historian, finding more than enough to do on the history of the library itself, grits his teeth and lets background matters go hang if there are no reputable monographs on them that he may conveniently pillage.

Quite often, even now, one may come across a town, or region, for which little acceptable work has been done on its social and economic history. Although local studies are in the ascendant, their popularity is so recent that there is a colossal amount of solid work still untouched. Furthermore, as J D Marshall has said, much of the work which is being done is in the hands of amateurs with insufficient guidance from the professionals. 'If academic studies and the social sciences', he said, 'tend steadily to become more fragmented, local history studies present an even more severe case of the same malady.' The problem now is, how may the results of specialisation be brought together to make a meaningful whole?(8)

Whatever the difficulties, the problem of background information must not be shirked. Unfortunately, the question we have to resolve is how much, or how little, we should be prepared to accept from a library historian who has had little time for research on background matters himself and has found there was little done by others he could adapt or adopt?

In a recorded conversation with David Gerard, Professor Kelly was even more forthright than he was in his published paper. 'Unless', he said, 'the history of an individual library can be related to the wider background, it ceases to have any real value.' Hard words, but worth remembering.(9)

What is just as bad as no background information at all is the provision of some background information in the early part of the history and no more thereafter. Thus, we are told that, in 1885 Barset was a town of 70,000 and its staple industries were the manufacture of hats, shoes and corsets; and that it had one theatre, many schools, chapels and churches, and even more public houses. The street-lighting was gas, the town was served by two railway companies, most of the houses were rented and the enfranchised section of the population was staunchly Liberal. The rest is silence. The town became frozen in time. The public library grew, but all else in Barset stood still.

VII

When all the research has been done on the history of a library and the task of writing the text has to be faced, the first problem to resolve is whether or not to follow a strict chronological pattern and the second, closely allied to it, is how to break up the text into convenient chapters or sections.

In a large-scale history, strict chronology is wearisome and confusing, both to the author and to his readers. Almost every topic becomes fragmented, facts come and go without making any impression, and comments make no impact because the facts to which they relate are scattered.

The best plan is, to identify the key events, such as the appointment and retirement of chief librarians, periods of war and recession, the removal to new premises, and break the course of the narrative according to them. Within these

58

divisions chronology can, and should, be made subservient to topics, such as finance, buildings, staff and services, which should be dealt with separately. It is essential, however, to compile a chronology for personal use. It might be helpful to the readers to provide a shortened version of this, before or after the text.

VIII

I end this chapter on a discouraging note. In his review of *Parnassus on Main Street*, John C Abbott said: 'Relative to their role as custodians of our cultural heritage, librarians, as a group, show remarkably little interest in their own history. This is another way of saying that library histories, particularly histories of individual libraries, are not likely to be widely read.'(10)   A survey of the collections on library science to which I most often resort suggests that Mr Abbott is right.

FOUR

THE BIOGRAPHICAL APPROACH

BIOGRAPHY occupies an equivocal position in the literary firmament. There is no general agreement as to whether it is an art or a craft, and only partial agreement as to what a biographer should aim at and what he should avoid.

Sixty years ago, Lytton Strachey introduced his *Eminent Victorians* to the public by condemning the traditional, long-winded biographies of celebrities, with their 'lamentable lack of selection, of detachment, of design'. Looking at what has happened to biography since Strachey, one thing is clear: his own precepts and examples notwithstanding, there is no guarantee that a short biography is any more likely to please than a long one. In America, in fact, the great American biography rates higher, in critical esteem, than the great American novel; witness Leon Edel's biography of Henry James and Leslie A Marchand's biography of Lord Byron.

But the greatest peculiarity of the current biographical scene is that one of its major features is a massive, two-volume biography of Strachey himself, by Michael Holroyd; this is about six times as long as Strachey's *Queen Victoria*.

Following the publication of his second major biography (of Augustus John), Holroyd reflected on the biographical art in the pages of *The times*. He called biography 'The child of the strange coupling between history and the novel', adding that 'in its recent development it has tended to resemble the latter.'(1)

Holroyd is not the only biographer who has tried to unveil the mysteries of his craft. The testimonies of several others who have done so have been collected by James L Clifford (himself a creditable biographer of Dr Samuel Johnson) in an anthology of considerable interest called *Biography as an art: selected criticism 1560-1960* (OUP, 1962).

To a reader with a liking for biographies, this is a beguiling volume. To a prospective biographer it is a recipe for confusion and alarm. Biography, he will be told, is 'the discovery of a human soul'. The biographer must neither suppress information, nor sit in judgment, but must study his subject with scientific detachment. Nevertheless, he must contrive to bring him to life. He must not ignore any source of information, but should sift his findings carefully, retaining only those that are true. He must leave 'a margin of contemporary facts' round his subject, but it must not be too wide, or his biography will be all 'times' and no 'life'. He must be readable, but wary of humour and 'the tincture of irony'.

The chances of writing a biography which is both a brilliant example of the art, and also a popular success, are small. Anyone who deliberately sought to gain this distinction is hardly likely to choose a librarian as his subject.

II

Biographies of librarians do exist, but they are quite unpopular. That the public should ignore them is no matter for surprise. The public will always be more inclined to read the life of a libertine than a librarian, whatever its literary merit. Casanova was both, but not (unfortunately for library biography) at the same time. He ended his days, in dreary respectability, as the librarian of a Bohemian nobleman.

To be fair, the public's prejudices are not always absurd. When the public finds more of interest in the life of an author than in the life of a publisher, and more of interest in the life of a publisher than in the life of a librarian, it does so because, in the work of a librarian, it can see neither mystery nor magic. An author is usually creative; a publisher, because he can discover, encourage, and sometimes even inspire authors, is occasionally creative; a librarian, as a mere custodian of the books which authors write and publishers commission, is not creative at all.

The unpopularity of librarians' biographies with the public is understandable. The public has only a vague idea, based on imperfect knowledge of what librarians do, as to why librarianship is a profession. What is much more disconcerting is that librarians' biographies should be unpopular with librarians. If Ambrose Bierce were alive today, to add a definition of 'library biography' to his notorious *Devil's dictionary*, it might read something like this:

Library biography. A well-intentioned, obligatory memorial to a librarian who was either great, or is believed to have been great. Its readership is small and does not greatly exceed those most closely associated with its production, namely, its author, publisher and printer. It may possibly be read, also, by its reviewers, but this cannot be depended upon. The first editions of library biographies are likely to lead long and peaceful lives, either in library stacks, or in publishers' warehouses. Second editions are extremely rare.

An apparent exception to this definition is *The life of Sir Anthony Panizzi KCB* by Louis Fagan (two volumes, Remington, 1880). Although scarcely a representative of 'light literature', either in length or style, this biography not only reached a second edition, but the first was exhausted within a week of publication. Naturally, the author was pleased, but his deprecating comment that this gratifying result was due 'less to the merit of the work than to the inherent interest of the subject' (who was hated at least as much as he was loved) was probably nearer the truth than he would have cared to admit.

Panizzi, by the way, is one of the few librarians for whom there is more than one biography. The second, if one counts only complete biographies, is *Prince of librarians* by Edward Miller (Deutsch, 1967). If Barbara McCrimmon is right, there is already a strong case for a third.(2) Melvil Dewey, no matter for surprise, is also the subject of two biographies, but still awaits a biographer with the talent and resolution to do him justice.

The small cluster of biographies of British librarians has two readily identifiable features: it is biassed towards librarians of public libraries (national and local) and a good part of it is the work of a single biographer, W A Munford.

Surprisingly, Dr Munford began his biographical career with a biography of William Ewart, a House of Commons back bencher who supported a number of worthy causes other than the establishment of public libraries. Dr Munford continued with a life of Edward Edwards which supplanted the pioneer biography by Thomas Greenwood, shared with W G Fry the agreeable task of writing 'a biographical sketch' of Louis Stanley Jast and lastly (but only for the time being, I hope) wrote a brief biography of James Duff Brown, the industrious reformer and teacher of public library economy, who achieved more than seemed possible in a life so short.(3)

Dr Munford's reflections on his unique experience as a library biographer have been recorded, with characteristic good humour, in his 'Confessions of a library biographer' *Library review* 21 (6) Summer 1968, 293-297. None of his four biographies has achieved the sale it deserved. The first had already been remaindered by the time the 'Confessions' were written, a doleful fate which its undaunted author cheerfully 'celebrated' in verse.

But neither then, nor since, has Dr Munford had regrets. The labour involved which, for this kind of work, must always be a labour of love, made him new friends and took him to new places. After listing the various libraries and record offices in which he had gathered materials he said: 'In each of them have come those ecstatic moments when one seems to have temporarily abandoned one's own workaday life and instead, feels as if re-living the career of a long-dead professional colleague',(4) an observation which can be matched by Michael Holroyd's: 'A biographer's life may have similarities with that of an actor. He must read, learn lines, metaphorically put on the clothes and become his subject—know what it is like to think, feel, move about the room like him.'(5)

III

At present, the American library profession is ahead of the British in honouring its great men and women. It has not only produced more full-length biographies, published and unpublished, but has recently produced a splendid gallery of miniature portraits of 302 men and women who have some claim to remembrance in American library history in the massive *Dictionary of American library biography* edited by

Bohdan S Wynar (Littleton, Colo; Libraries Unlimited, 1978). This is not only valuable in its own right as a biographical dictionary, but, by virtue of its careful documentation, offers an instant indication of what has been done, and therefore of what remains to be done, on the lives of all the persons included. Nothing of this kind exists for British librarians, although Dr Munford has declared, in the foreword to his centennial *A history of the Library Association 1877-1977* (Library Association, 1976) that he hopes to publish a biographical dictionary of British librarians 'during the early years of the Association's second century'.

The American library profession has done something else which has no counterpart in Great Britain: it has honoured several of its great librarians of the past by publishing selections from their professional writings, supported by bibliographies and short biographies. Good examples are *Selected papers of John Shaw Billings* compiled by Frank Bradway Rogers (Medical Library Association, 1965) and *Charles Ammi Cutter: library systematizer* edited by Francis L Miksa (Littleton, Colo; Libraries Unlimited, 1977). The latter volume is one of a series of such compilations published by Libraries Unlimited. The general editor is Michael H Harris; the series is called 'The heritage of librarianship'.

IV
It is possible, of course, to write a purely professional biography of a librarian. Sometimes, unfortunately, it is difficult, if not impossible, to do anything else. When a distinguished librarian devoted most of his time to his work, or when almost the only records left are of his professional activities, the biographer must do the best he can and hope his readers will not complain.

When Fielding Garrison wrote his admirable biography of John Shaw Billings, soldier, surgeon, and expert on public health, hospital construction and medical education, as well as a distinguished librarian, he was fortunate, as he was able to enliven his narrative with quotations from a marvellous file of letters which Billings had written to his wife whenever his engagements took him away from home. The warmth of his affection, and his sharp and humorous observations, are a welcome relief from the more solemn passages of the biography describing his professional activities. After a spell of fishing in Canadian rivers he wrote: 'My right arm aches and I can't write that beautiful copper plate hand which you admire so much, but I feel very fine, and several inches larger in every direction.' On another occasion he wrote from a freezing Vienna: 'It is still cold and damp and raw, very depressing weather for sight-seers, the picture galleries are mostly not heated and the few people who visit them go shivering around over the stone floors with cold feet and red noses, and hurry through with the show as fast as possible. There are many statues in the open places through the city, but they have all got snow wigs on and look as if a good fire under them would help things a good deal.'(6)

The main difficulties encountered when writing the biography of a librarian, apart from the literary skill needed to imbue the portrait with some semblance of life, are accumulating the relevant materials and effectively deploying them. A hazard which is much less common, I hope, than my own limited experience in the biographical field suggests, is the dearth of private papers. This is mostly due to the destructive activities of the subject's family, who sometimes fail to realise his importance in the history of his profession. Another possibility, which is rather more exasperating, is one I encountered when working on my biography of Ernest A Savage.

Savage was a forceful personality, as his writings show, and highly critical of the work of others. He was also the most original mind in British public librarianship between the two world wars. At some time during his retirement, like his favourite author, Dickens, he had an 'ante-mortem bonfire' of his books and papers. Into it, as he coolly recorded, went 'all private letters in my hands'.(7) The irony of this is that Savage was a zealous library historian whose last writings on library history were produced after this woeful blaze.

It would seem from the notes on 'primary sources and archival materials' appended to the articles in the *Dictionary of American library biography* that many records relating to distinguished American librarians have been preserved; although, predictably, there have been some losses. Francis

L Miksa says that the personal papers of Charles Ammi Cutter were destroyed on the death of Mrs Cutter, and Michael H Harris reports that few of Charles Coffin Jewett's letters have survived. William Landram Williamson was obliged to write his excellent biography *William Frederick Poole and the modern library movement* (New York: Columbia University Press, 1963) with few of Poole's private papers. 'It is almost inexplicable', said Edward G Holley in his review, 'that some of the chief figures in librarianship felt so little need to preserve their private correspondence.'(8)

By contrast, when Maurice F Tauber set about writing *Louis Round Wilson: librarian and administrator* (New York: Columbia University Press, 1967), his subject was still alive and gave his biographer cordial help. (In 1976 he performed an even rarer office: he helped celebrate his own centennial.)

V

The librarians of the past whose names come most readily to mind are the titans of the profession; men and women who devoted most of their lives to librarianship, sometimes notching up more than fifty years of service. There are several interesting exceptions—librarians who, by accident or design, were in librarianship for only a short time, but still managed to make their mark. A particularly good example is Miss A S Cooke (1895-1971), first county librarian of Kent, who created a thriving library service out of limited resources, but left the profession, for personal reasons, at the age of forty-seven.(9)

It should hardly be necessary to say that talent and distinction in librarianship have not been the prerogative of the chiefs of the larger libraries. I myself have known several librarians of small libraries who were as competent and as dedicated as a librarian could be. Some librarians of small public libraries, for example, chose to remain with them as they had become so identified with their readers and their communities that they had lost all desire to frog-hop across the country in search of the better paid posts. A good example, brought to my notice by one of my students, is J T Houghton (1870-1936), for many years librarian of the small town of Worksop, in Nottinghamshire. During this time, he won for his library a permanent place in the history of British library co-operation, by carrying out, virtually single-handed, an experimental scheme funded by the Carnegie United Kingdom Trust, to provide books to villages in the county, in order to demonstrate that a county library service was feasible. 'The Worksop experiment', which sounds oddly like a science-fiction story by H G Wells, is one of the many bright fragments of library history well worth preserving.(10)

VI

Librarianship, like every profession, has had its black sheep, and also, what is rather more relevant to a discussion of the need for library biographies, its black and white sheep—by which I mean those librarians who may truly be said to have fallen from grace, as they had attained a state of grace to fall from. In accord with the present-day inclination to forgive and remember, rather than to curse and forget, the library profession has latterly re-instated some of its black and white sheep.

The pre-eminent example is Klas August Linderfelt (1847-1900), an American librarian of Swedish origin, once famous for his *Eclectic card catalog rules*, whose forced resignation from the presidency of the American Library Association, in 1892, for embezzlement while librarian of Milwaukee, was made retrospective to the date of his election to the office, in 1891! Quite properly, Linderfelt, warts and all, has a place in the new *Dictionary of American library biography*. His sponsor is Wayne A Wiegand, who has written about him at greater length elsewhere. (11)

The English librarian Henry Bond (1871-1917) has less claim to distinction, as a librarian, but his story is more tragic. Having had his salary as chief librarian of St Pancras reduced from £400 to £200 a year, for no better reason than that a newly elected Borough Council was resolved to annihilate a scheme to provide St Pancras with a comprehensive library service, which an earlier Council had approved, Bond tried to recoup his losses, when he moved on to Portsmouth Public Libraries, by ingeniously robbing the book-fund. When discovery became imminent, he took his life.

At the time of his death he was honorary editor (admittedly with rather restricted powers) of the *Library Association record*. Bond has a peculiar interest as a man of only moderate ability whose life is, nevertheless, worth investigating because of the affairs (of the Library Association and St Pancras) in which he was involved.(12)

VII

For every full-length library biography there must be at least twenty biographical essays. Some are in encyclopaedias, others in biographical dictionaries, a few in *Festschriften*, many in periodicals, a fair number, especially obituaries, in newspapers. In short, biographical essays on librarians (and distinguished laymen in library history) are widely scattered, and so offer a considerable challenge to some library history anthologist of the future, who will undoubtedly find at least a few vignettes worth salvaging.

The biographical essay, save where it is written to a set pattern, as for a biographical dictionary, has considerable attraction for the prospective biographer. But, as many a library school student, slaving over a biographical 'project', has discovered, it can prove unexpectedly difficult. An essay of 5,000 words on a librarian, if it is to be a good essay, will involve more than a tenth of the labour required for a 50,000 word biography. Beginning from scratch, with little or no prior knowledge of the subject, the task of finding enough materials for a balanced short biography can be quite considerable. This is supposing, of course, that the essay is to cover the entire life of the subject; but it is a proper, but not sufficiently common, device to use the essay form to concentrate on one particular phase of the subject's career. K A Manley has done this effectively in his valuable essay 'E B Nicholson and the London Institution' *Journal of librarianship* 5 (1) January 1973, 55-77, all the more welcome because it deals with the history of an institution which has long since disappeared and an episode in the career of a remarkable personality who is too often remembered solely as one of Bodley's librarians.

A type of biographical essay which is too little practised in Britain is the informed study which is based on intimate knowledge, sometimes personal knowledge, but free from editorial guide-lines and the tyranny of notes and references. A biographical essay which is written out of many years' acquaintance with the subject is more likely to have the glow of life than one whose only warmth is of the midnight oil.

Some of the best American examples are the texts of papers delivered at meetings of the Library History Round Table, among them Margery Doud 'Recollections of Arthur E Bostwick' and Emily Miller Danton 'Mr ALA—Carl Hastings Milam', both of which have been reprinted in *An American library history reader* selected by John David Marshall (Hamden, Conn; Shoe String Press, 1961).

British examples which come to mind are W A Munford 'Portrait of a woman librarian: Ethel Winifred Austin' *Library world* 60 (705) March 1959, 166-170 and Ernest A Savage 'James Duff Brown after fifty years' *Library review* 17 (135) Autumn 1960, 489-495.

All these have one thing in common, apart from their merit as biographical sketches. Short as they are, they show the strength of the hold which librarianship exerts on those who serve it well.

As the bookman-librarian seems to have given place to the document manipulator, the following extract from 'I once did see Joe Wheeler plain' by Margaret A Edwards *Journal of library history* 6 (4) October 1971, 291-302 may seem old-fashioned, but it brings a great librarian vividly to life: 'Books excited him and he was daily in the order department laying his hands reverently on the new books, for any one of them, he often said, might change the plans and life of whoever read it.'

A particular virtue of the biographical essay is that it can be used to pay tribute to librarians whose merits would be obscured, rather than illuminated, by a full-length biography. Such a man was Charles Hocking (c. 1885-1965), the conscientious, hard-working librarian of the London Borough of Acton. Recalling him in 'They kept libraries going' *New library world* 78 (930) December 1977, 233-234, Bernard Palmer summed up his special qualities in the remark, 'He saw things through in hard times.'

VIII

The substantial growth of the library profession during the present century has meant a greater number of deaths to mourn, a greater number of obituaries to write. One inevitable result of this has been a reduction in the space devoted to the obituaries of the more outstanding members. In 1914, the *Library Association record* devoted twenty-four pages to obituary notices of James Duff Brown. In 1945, the *Library world* devoted twelve pages to appreciations of L Stanley Jast. As tributes on this scale are no longer welcome by the editors of the periodicals on librarianship, the case for separately published biographies of eminent librarians is all the greater.

On the other hand, obituaries have gained, in recent years, from a greater measure of frankness and informality. When Septimus A Pitt, city librarian of Glasgow, died in office in 1937, his friend Ernest A Savage, chiefly remembered for his caustic frankness, wrote an obituary notice of him which praised him unreservedly as 'an organiser and administrator of the highest capacity, sure in judgment, resolute in purpose, calm and confident in manner', and as a man whose reticence screened the kindest of hearts.

By contrast, F G B Hutchings, who worked as a junior under Pitt, recalled him, in 1974, as a man absolutely fixed in his habits, one who worked in 'a pre-destined groove', and the kind of chief who bore so heavily on his staff that a great wave of relief spread through the library on the days when his engagements took him away from it. 'He had the power of God over us', said Hutchings, in a tart observation which could be applied to many of the chiefs of earlier generations. Somewhere, between the testimonies of the old friend and the young junior subordinate, must lie the real Septimus A Pitt.

When J P Lamb, one-time city librarian of Sheffield, died in 1969, Philip Hepworth neatly accounted for both his virtues and his weaknesses: 'He hated laziness, pretension, university libraries and London public libraries.' This he did, as I have reason to know.

'Obituaries of librarians' according to W A Munford, 'are frequently indifferently well done.' It is true that the

71

average standard of obituaries in our profession is not very high in comparison with some others. But granted the speed with which, too often, they have to be written, they are sometimes remarkably good. Two recent examples which will bear anthologising one day are 'Stanley Snaith: a memoir' by K C Harrison *New library world* 78 (925) July 1977, 125-126, an affectionate portrait of a public librarian who was also a poet and a wit; and 'F G B Hutchings' by W B P [W B Paton] *Library Association record* 80 (7) July 1978, 365-367—a perfect memorial and a well deserved tribute to a gifted, exuberant, warm-hearted personality, who served for some years as city librarian of Leeds, and when he might have retired, shared his knowledge and experience with the students of several schools of librarianship, at home and abroad.

IX

There is as much still to do in the realm of library biography as anywhere in library history. In Britain, some of the more obvious gaps are among the biographies of university and special librarians. For Cambridge there are the two unduly neglected biographies *Henry Bradshaw* by G W Prothero (Kegan Paul, 1888) and *Francis Jenkinson* by H F Stewart (Cambridge University Press, 1926); for Oxford there is *E W B Nicholson (1849-1912)* by K A Manley, an Oxford thesis biography of a talented eccentric who was the virtual founder of the Library Association as well as one of the more notable of Bodley's librarians.

For Oxford and Cambridge, these may be regarded as the minimum biographical coverage of university librarians. For the modern universities, we have not reached even that stage. It is true that, until the eve of the Victorian age, there were no universities in England and Wales other than Oxford and Cambridge, and that the libraries of the new 'redbrick' universities were, for many years, short of funds, except for the occasional benefaction. But one has only to read the paper by John Wilks, *The influence of R W Chambers on the development of university libraries* (H K Lewis for University College, London, 1953) to realise that we are in danger of over-emphasising public librarians in our professional roll of honour.

72

In special libraries, few in number and mostly small in resources, in Britain, until the middle of the present century, the likely candidates for full biographies seem to be few. One who is certainly worthy of the honour is the legendary Dr S C Bradford, librarian of the Science Museum, who appreciated the need for a National Lending Library for Science and Technology long before there was one. Bradford is vividly recalled by D J Urquhart and M Gosset in a symposium on him published in the *Journal of documentation* 33 (3) September 1977, 173-179.

There is one other limitation to library biography in Britain. In the USA, library biography has paid due attention to those librarians who made their names not as chief librarians, but as specialists in subordinate positions, eg Charles Martel, head of the Library of Congress Catalog Division and architect of the Library of Congress Classification; Isadore Gilbert Mudge, reference librarian, Columbia University Library; and Anne Carroll Moore, Superintendent of Work with Children, New York Public Library. For Miss Moore there is a charming full-scale biography which has actually been published on both sides of the Atlantic: *Anne Carroll Moore: a biography* by Frances Clarke Sayers (New York: Atheneum Publishers, 1972; Hamish Hamilton, 1972).

Until recent years, however, it was unusual for British librarians to make their names as specialist subordinates, as too few such posts existed and where they did the salaries were poor. Hence, the way ahead, for most recruits to the library profession, was the hard road to the top. Among the few exceptions was Herbert Woodbine, chief assistant and reference librarian, Birmingham City Libraries, recalled by Allan Whatley in 'Reference back: Herbert Woodbine, reference librarian and bibliographer' *Library review* 25 (5-6) Spring-Summer 1976, 181-187; and Frederick James Cox, legendary guardian of the issue desk at the London Library, like Woodbine, a superb bookman-librarian. When Cox died, he was accorded the signal honour of an obituary notice in *The times*, August 25th 1955.

It is arguable also, that in both Britain and America too little attention has been paid to the lay supporters of libraries, apart from outstanding figures such as Sir Thomas Bodley, Thomas Greenwood, Andrew Carnegie and H W Wilson.

Among the chairmen of library committees and boards there have been men and women well worth remembering who seem to have been forgotten, even locally. There are one or two who are remembered, unfortunately, for the harm they did. To find a library's greatest enemy on its own committee is the saddest of ironies, but such cases are not unknown.(13)

X

Autobiographies of librarians are, as yet, quite few, and most of those which have been published are American. The dangers involved in writing library history of this kind are obvious. To play down one's own achievements is as dishonest as to magnify them. Worse still, how may one account for one's contemporaries?

If Stanley Jast had been asked to write his autobiography I suspect he would have refused. There was something of the artist, particularly the actor, in Jast. He loved the limelight and he aimed to please. His friend, and former colleague, Ernest A Savage, had no compunction about exposing the failings of former colleagues and acquaintances and he did so quite heartily in *A librarian's memories* (Grafton, 1952). Jast contented himself with an amusing autobiographical essay, well buried in the files of a defunct periodical, but worth seeking out: 'A public library in the eighties' *Librarian* 24 (5) January 1935, 131-133.

Despite its imperfections, its incompleteness as a record of Savage's personal and public life, and its unjustifiably caustic portrait of Henry Tedder, librarian of the London Athenaeum and honorary treasurer of the Library Association, Savage's autobiography is far more profitable reading than Fremont Rider's *And master of none* (Middleton, Conn; Godey Memorial Library, 1955). This is subtitled 'an autobiography in the third person', which is quite accurate—and, therefore, discouraging, to begin with. 'Whatever the final result is', said Rider in his preface (which he called 'By way of preface'), 'I enormously enjoyed the doing of it.' His enjoyment is not communicated to the reader. The autobiography of Louis Shores is little better. Entitled *Quiet world: a librarian's crusade for destiny* (Hamden, Conn;

Linnet Books, 1975) it depicts the author as a kind of library missionary in a rather unendearing way.

Perhaps the most successful librarian's autobiography is Lawrence Clark Powell's *Fortune and friendship* (New York: Bowker, 1968) which Michael H Harris described aptly as 'written in the same confident vein in which the author conducted his life'.

It is likely, however, that when all the full-scale autobiographies of the great men of librarianship have been forgotten, an unpretentious autobiographical fragment by a British children's librarian will survive. I refer to Eileen Colwell's *How I became a librarian* (Nelson, 1956). Savage was obviously conscious of the importance of being Savage, Rider of being Rider, Shores of being Shores. Miss Colwell, for all that she was a children's librarian of international renown, was more conscious of the privilege and the opportunities she had had to serve her readers. Her book was written for a 'How I became' series, in which she had to compete for attention with a ballet dancer, a nursing sister, an engine driver and a detective. She more than held her own. Services to children, like much else, developed very slowly in Britain. What conditions were like at the point when, in a few libraries, they really began to develop, is told with humour and a kindly frankness which admirably testify to Miss Colwell's well-known skill as a story-teller.

Here, for once, is a contribution to library history in which library readers have a place. For example:
'The children's faith that I had read all the books in the library was implicit. A small boy asked me one day, 'Have you read this book, miss?'
'No,' I replied.
'Have you read this one?'
'No, I'm afraid I haven't', I answered, feeling quite apologetic.
'You're not much good, are you miss?' said the boy scathingly, and I humbly agreed I wasn' ' (p 66-67).

XI

As the biographical approach to history is, for many people, the most agreeable approach, the small circulation of those biographies of notabilities in library history which have been published leads one to make the awful speculation 'Is the lack of interest due to lack of appeal in the biographers or the biographees?'

Although there is no André Maurois, Harold Nicolson, or Leon Edel among the ranks of library biographers, there is a decent level of competence in their work which compares well enough with the biographies of notabilities in other professions. As to the subjects of library biographies, it is only necessary to dip into the *Dictionary of American library biography* to discover, should it be necessary, that the lives of librarians are not the apotheosis of monotony. Therefore, could it be that the trouble with biographies of librarians is that they are mostly written by librarians? that library biography, like the rest of library history, is too inbred?

The first challenge to library biography is to interest the library profession at large. The second is to interest the public. Neither is near to being met.

FIVE

COMPILING AND EDITING

ANYONE who is really anxious to contribute to the literature of library history will find, sooner or later, something agreeable to do. Compiling and editing may seem far from agreeable. Thomas Kelly has said that all work on library history includes a high proportion of drudgery. But undeniably, in compiling and editing, the drudgery is greater, and the literary skill smaller, than in the composition of essays and monographs. Nevertheless, compiling and editing have their own importance. At best they do, in fact, offer scope for the creative instinct, and there are some who would rather undertake work of this kind than try to hammer out a flawless historical narrative.

Among the tasks which await those who have the energy and the inclination to compile, accumulate, annotate and index are the editing of reprints, the recording of oral history and the compilation of reference works and bibliographies.

Editing reprints
A publishing phenomenon of the post-war years which librarians regard with mixed feelings is the reprinting, either in volume form or as microtexts, of out-of-print books of potential value for study and research. This often means a straightforward reproduction of the original text and nothing more. There are occasions, however, when it would be a great advantage to augment the original text with notes and other editorial matter. Sometimes, in fact, it would be a boon to provide a feature that the original document should have had in the first place—an index. These additions are particularly desirable for reprints of the governmental and other reports which are as prominent in the history of libraries as they are in every other area of social history.

Thanks to the College of Librarianship Wales, three famous reports on British public libraries were reprinted by Uniersity Microfilms, in book-form, several years ago, namely: *A report on library provision and policy by Professor W G S Adams to the Carnegie United Kingdom Trustees* (Dunfermline: Carnegie United Kingdom Trust, 1915), known as the Adams Report; the Board of Education Public Libraries Committee *Report on public libraries in England and Wales* (HMSO, 1927), known as the Kenyon Report; and Lionel R McColvin *The public library system of Great Britain: a report on its present condition with proposals for post-war re-organisation* (Library Association, 1942), known as the McColvin Report. As all three reports had been out-of-print for some years, their republication was welcome.

But there is still a need for edited editions of them, for reasons not hard to find. Firstly, how and why were these reports commissioned? Secondly, how were they received when they were published? Thirdly, what known or probable effect did they have on public library development in Britain? Fourthly, who were the men and women who, singly or jointly, compiled and drafted these reports? Lionel McColvin is still remembered; so, perhaps, is Sir Frederic Kenyon; but who was Professor Adams, and who were W R Barker, Frank Pacy and Lady Mabel Smith, all of whom served on the Kenyon Committee?

As an alternative to publishing an edited edition of a report, a bare reprint could be accompanied by a separately published 'companion'. This helpful device was used in connection with the reprint of the classic Williamson Report on library education in the USA. *Training for library service* (1923), prepared by Charles C Williamson for the Carnegie Corporation of New York, was based on an earlier, unpublished report by Dr Williamson, called *Training for library work* (1921). This preliminary report has been first published, and the 1923 report reprinted, together in one volume; and an original commentary on both reports in another: *The Williamson Reports of 1921 and 1923* (Metuchen NJ: Scarecrow Press, 1971) and Sarah K Vann *The Williamson Reports: a study* (Metuchen NJ: Scarecrow Press, 1971).

Oral history

Oral history is not a new phenomenon. The practice of discovering, questioning and recording the eyewitnesses of events goes back to Herodotus. But the term 'oral history' is new. New, also, are the discussions of its techniques and purpose and the use of sophisticated recording apparatus. There are now oral history societies, oral history journals and oral history manuals. Among the latter are two which, though quite different, are both worth looking at; namely, Paul Thompson *The voice of the past: oral history* (OUP, 1978), a comprehensive manual on the nature, value and practice of library history, and Cullan Davis, Kathryn Back and Kay MacLean *Oral history: from tape to type* (Chicago: American Library Association, 1977), a useful self-instruction manual.

Paul Thompson is a great enthusiast for oral history because he believes 'it can give back to the people who made and experienced history' a central place in history through their own recorded words. Although there must be many librarians who are aware of oral history, few seem to have bothered to apply it to library history. There are a few tape recordings in the Library Association Library (now part of the British Library) but, at the time of writing, neither the Library Association nor the LA Library has an active oral history programme.

The major oral contribution to library history in the United Kingdom has come from David Gerard, senior lecturer, College of Librarianship Wales, Aberystwyth, who has built up for the College an admirable collection of tape recordings of many distinguished British librarians, among them Sir Frank Francis (former Director and Principal Librarian of the British Museum), Lionel McColvin (former city librarian of Westminster and honorary secretary of the Library Association), J N L Myres (formerly one of Bodley's librarians) and the late F G B Hutchings (former city librarian of Leeds and President of the Library Association). There are also recordings of three distinguished library historians, who need no further introduction, Raymond Irwin, Thomas Kelly and W A Munford.

Although there is an article on oral history in the *Encyclopedia of library and information science*, it has nothing to say about its application to library history. The several references to oral history in the *Journal of library history* have also been mainly on oral history at large, not on oral history in the cause of library history. What has actually been done by library historians in the USA in this direction is not clear.

Two matters which must not be overlooked when library historians do pay attention to oral history is the need to secure recordings from the rank and file of the library profession, and also from a cross-section of library users. Just how much testimonies such as these would enliven the histories of individual libraries has still, I believe, to be demonstrated. Just as, when map-making, one needs sightings from more than one position, so also, when investigating the history of a library, one needs the view from more than one vantage point.

When J P Lamb retired from the chiefship of Sheffield city libraries in 1956, the entire Summer issue of the staff magazine *Spellbound*, was devoted to reminiscences and appreciations of him and of the city libraries. It was vaguely known by all of us that in the old days, life in the city libraries was crude and rough; but it was a retired branch librarian, Mr T E Osborn, who made us realise how crude, and how rough, in a vivid contribution which included passages such as these:

It was a regular occurrence to call in the police to maintain order, especially on Sundays, and it was no strange occurrence to be chased by gangs of young toughs into the police station in Whitworth Lane after closing.

There was no staff room at the central library and meals were taken in the basement of the old building. We did not lack company, either, for there were plenty of mice, cockroaches and crickets to keep us from feeling lonely in that gas-lit dungeon.

There was no staff library, or any facilities for study. Indeed, studying for Library Association qualifications was frowned on by the authorities.

'The voice of the past matters to the present', says Paul

Thompson, adding 'But whose voice—or voices—are to be heard?'

Illustrations
1977 was a good year for library history in Great Britain, largely because it was the centennial of the Library Association. Among the several volumes on British library history published then were Thomas Kelly and Edith Kelly *Books for the people: an illustrated history of the British public library* (Deutsch, 1977) and Alan W Ball *The public libraries of Greater London: a pictorial history 1856-1914* (Library Association London and Home Counties Branch, 1977). Although widely different in style and scope, these useful and attractive volumes have in common a feature unusual in the literature of library history: they are lavishly illustrated. Should there by any doubt as to whether illustrations can be of any value in the history of libraries, whether they can, to any degree, strengthen a text, and not merely decorate it, these books should dispel it. Mr Ball's subject was more specific than Mrs Kelly's and he was more fortunate in his discoveries. Although he occasionally departed from it, Mr Ball's main object was to depict the early years of the public libraries of Greater London with the aid of as wide a variety of illustrations as possible. He was unexpectedly successful. The range and quality of the illustrations, and the light-hearted but shrewdly informative captions, together made a fascinating volume which won the approval of, among others, Sir John Betjeman.

Faced with the task of finding illustrations for a library history of a scope much wider, both in time and place, Mrs Kelly's major problem, you might think, would have been one of choice. Unfortunately, the negligence which has whittled away the printed and manuscript records of a number of our public libraries has also depleted the stock of their pictorial records as well; although 'depleted' is probably not the whole truth of the matter. Some public libraries, I feel certain, never had many photographs to lose, or discard, in the first place. Almost certainly, this reflects both the poverty, and with it the lack of pride, which afflicted British public libraries for so many years.

I need no pictures to remind me of the shabby public rooms of the central library where I began my library career, but I would be glad to know that some exist. The written records show that libraries, overall, have progressed, but they do not adequately show the conditions they have progressed from. A point of interest here is that sometimes you may discover excellent photographs of the interior of a library when it was clean and bright from the builder's hands, but the rooms are either quite deserted, or show only civic or academic bigwigs, in gilded robes or Sunday best. No readers are in sight. Why photograph *them*? What credit did they bring to a neo-Gothic masterpiece?

With illustrations, as with other library records, the only advice I can give to the explorer is to hope for the best but be prepared for the worst. It would be pleasant to record that the Library Association has taken the lead in the preservation of pictorial records, but it has not. Conference photographs one would have expected it to have are not in its files and not long since I discovered portraits of some of its past distinguished officers in a remote corner of the stationery store of its headquarters.

To end on a more cheerful note, I cordially recommend a delightful essay by A E Day, 'Bibliothecal deltiology' *Library review* 25 (8) Winter 1976-1977, 318-322, which discusses the gentle art, or science, of collecting picture postcards of libraries.

Reference works
There are no encyclopaedias of library history. In theory there could be, say, *An Oxford companion to library history*, or even *A dictionary of British/American library history*, but no works of this kind are in sight. For want of them, a good deal of time has to be spent searching for simple facts in scattered sources of information, including periodicals. For those engaged on theses and dissertations this is probably regarded as part of the exercise. After all, it swells the references and bibliographies and is, therefore, worthy of credit. But the duplication of effort is wasteful. There is not much, however, the lone compiler can do in this area.

The scope and excellence of the *Dictionary of American library biography* shows very clearly that major reference works on library history had better be team works. But the annotated list of sources of information on library history in chapter six shows that some useful work has been done by lone compilers. The wider the extension of the work, the more difficult and dangerous it becomes. Even the chronology of a single library can be a major task; see, for example, W D Macray *Annals of the Bodleian Library, Oxford* (2nd edition, OUP, 1890).

Bibliographies
Although bibliographies are often reference works, the familiar phrase 'reference works and bibliographies' suggests that encyclopaedias, dictionaries, atlases and other non-bibliographical reference works are commonly regarded as one coherent group, and bibliographies as another.

In library history, the need for bibliographies has already been recognised (especially in the USA), but a good deal of work still needs to be done. In Britain, the major objective should be not only to continue the Library Association Library History Group's *British library history bibliography*, but to carry it back beyond 1962, where it begins.

In the USA, in addition to the recently published *American library history bibliography* (see chapter six) there is a series of state bibliographies sponsored by the *Journal of library history*. An impressive example is Doris Cruger Dale (ed) *Bibliography of Illinois library history* Journal of library history bibliography no 14 (Tallahassee: Journal of Library History and School of Library Science, Florida State University, 1976). Although it covers items written before 1972, it lists no less than 2,109, spread over 1,193 authors.

This series suggests that there is a case in Britain for regional bibliographies. There is certainly a case for author bibliographies, covering both the professional and the non-professional writings of notable librarians. So little work of this kind has been done so far in Britain that the need for it has obviously been scarcely considered. One of the few examples extant, and a good one, except that it is not annotated, is Joan Harris and R W Pound 'A bibliography of J H P Pafford' *in Libraries and literature: essays in honour of Jack Pafford* edited by A T Milne (University of London Athlone Press, 1970) 126-141.

In the USA, author bibliographies of librarians are much commoner; although, as they are usually concealed bibliographies, this is not obvious. Once again the *Journal of library history* provides an example: Mary Robinson Sive 'Helen E Haines 1872-1961: an annotated bibliography' *Journal of library history* 5 (2) April 1970, 146-164.

The compilation of author bibliographies is not as straightforward as it may seem. This is because the general bibliographies of librarianship cannot be relied upon to have picked up everything. Items published anonymously and pseudonymously, in local journals of librarianship, in newspapers and in non-library periodicals, can lead the bibliographer a merry dance. If there is a law of serendipity, in its application to the bibliography of librarianship it is a capricious law. Two items I would have been pleased to have known about many years before I lighted upon them I mention here, as they may be of interest to others:

Savage, Ernest A 'The public library service of Great Britain and Ireland' *in Year book of education 1933* (Evans, 1932) 286-298.

This brilliant essay by a master librarian and a forceful writer was eventually brought to my attention because someone who had come across it had had the wit to present a photocopy of it to the Library Association Library and the staff had catalogued it.

Jast, L Stanley 'Public libraries' *in A century of municipal progress: the last hundred years* edited by Harold J Laski, W Ivor Jennings and William A Robson (Allen & Unwin, 1935) 244-259.

This was brought to my attention by a colleague searching the stack of the university library for information on public health legislation in Victorian Britain.

Whether or not the author bibliography of a librarian should be absolutely complete must be decided on its merits. Some librarians (the late W C Berwick Sayers is a ready example) have been fluent to the point of garrulity.

SIX

REFERENCE AIDS TO STUDY AND RESEARCH

A SURE WAY of determining whether or not a subject has depth, as well as breadth, is to survey the principal sources of information on it. If they include reference works and periodicals, in addition to monographs, then the subject must have reached a state of appreciable substance and probably, also, of importance. I say 'probably', because nowadays one may find reference works and periodicals on subjects which many people would not regard as all that important, among them crime fiction and health foods.

The least we can say about library history is that it seems to be important, as it now boasts a small number of quick-reference sources of information which are undeniably useful and there are indications that others will shortly follow. There are also several works which are marginally useful for the information they contain relating to library history. All these publications are listed and briefly described below under the following headings:

Encyclopaedia
Yearbook
Chronologies
Biographical dictionaries
Periodicals
Bibliographies
Published library catalogues

The following abbreviations have been used to indicate the scope of the publications listed with regard to library history:

G : library history generally
B : wholly or mainly on British library history
A : wholly or mainly on American library history

Encyclopaedia
G 1 *Encyclopedia of library and information science*
New York: Marcel Dekker. vols 1-26 (A-S), 1968-
1979; in progress.

The virtues and defects of this encyclopaedia have been
carefully assessed by E V Corbett in his omnibus review of
volumes 1-18 in the *Journal of librarianship* 9 (2) April 1977
148-155. The *Encyclopedia* is international in scope, but
slanted towards the USA. It was inevitable that the articles
should vary in quality: this defect is almost impossible to
overcome in encyclopaedias, but it was not inevitable that
some topics should have been overlooked, or dealt with after
the most appropriate volumes for them had gone to press.

Library history is widely but unevenly represented. Until
the *Encyclopedia* is complete, and a master index available,
only page-by-page scanning will reveal those articles, or
sections of articles, which are specifically historical. There
are general articles on 'Library historiography' (remarkably
unconcerned with modern developments), 'Ancient and
medieval libraries', 'Roman and Greek libraries', 'Monastic
libraries' and 'Public libraries, International: history of the
public library'. There are also articles on the great libraries of
the world and their histories, but of random length. The
Bodleian Library has five pages and the Cambridge University
Library twenty; the Library Company of Philadelphia eight-
een pages and the London Library none. The same observation applies to the articles on the major library associations
and periodicals on librarianship. The *Encyclopedia* also
includes biographical articles. On these, see item 7 below.

Yearbook
A 2 *The ALA yearbook : a review of library events*,
1976 to date, Chicago: American Library Association, 1977 to date.

An illustrated, encyclopaedic annual register of library
progress, mainly in the USA, comprising a few long lead
articles, followed by numerous short articles in alphabetical
subject order. In a sense, all the articles are of historical
interest, but note particularly those on 'American library
history', the 'American Library History Round Table' and
'Obituaries'.

86

B   3   Thornton, John L *The chronology of librarianship: an introduction to the history of libraries and book-collecting* Grafton, 1941.

This work is in two parts. The first is a summary history of librarianship, the second is a bare chronology, from ancient times to 1938. The modern sections of both parts are slanted towards Great Britain. Links between scattered information on individual topics are provided by the detailed index. Although in need of revision, as well as of extension, this work is still of occasional use. The introduction, worth reading, is by Ernest A Savage.

B   4   Munford, W A (ed) *Annals of the Library Association 1877 to 1960* Library Association, 1965.

These *Annals* were started by Ernest A Savage (one time Honorary Secretary, later President, of the Library Association) who compiled and updated them for the 1930's editions of the *Library Association yearbook*. For this separately published edition they were extended to 1960 by Catherine Dowden, and edited by W A Munford, on behalf of the LA Library History Group. As many investigations into modern British library history involve references to the history of the LA and its branches, sections and groups, and sometimes to the history of the formerly independent library associations which the LA absorbed round about 1930, this chronology is of more value than may be supposed. It can now be used in conjunction with W A Munford *A history of the Library Association 1877-1977* (Library Association, 1976).

A   5   Smith, Josephine Metcalfe *A chronology of librarianship* Metuchen NJ: Scarecrow Press, 1968.

Although it begins with the first century AD, as the compiler admits in her preface, 'this chronology emphasises librarianship in the United States'. Entries are brief and sometimes of little importance in a library history chronology, eg, '1906 : The first reputed "blurb" appears on a book jacket', and although references are given to sources of information, they are often secondary sources. Nevertheless, Elizabeth W Stone, whose own chronology is vastly superior (see item 6), found some favour in this work. (See her review in the *Journal of library history* 4 (3) July 1969, 281-284.)

A   6   Stone, Elizabeth W *American library development 1600-1899* New York: H W Wilson, 1977.
A skeleton chart of American library history is followed by a detailed, well documented chronology, in which some entries extend to more than one page. The actual chronology is divided into eight separate sections: Private, special and government libraries; Academic libraries—school libraries; Public libraries; Technical services; Legislation; Publications; Professional activities; Buildings and miscellaneous. This is an unusually good chronology whose only significant defect is that its slender index does not do justice to the considerable amount of information in the text.

Biographical dictionaries
G   7   *Encyclopedia of library and information science* New York: Marcel Dekker. vols 1-26 (A-S), 1968-1979; in progress.
The biographical articles on American and British librarians are fairer to the former than the latter. James Duff Brown is in, but Louis Stanley Jast is not. Samuel Brown is in, but must be looked for under 'Itinerating libraries'. The longest biographical entry is for the Indian librarian S R Ranganathan, although Melvil Dewey and Sir Anthony Panizzi are not far behind. Some notabilities have been overlooked and others excluded because they were still alive when the volumes which might have covered them were published. These will be included in the *Encyclopedia's* supplementary volumes.

A one volume encyclopaedia of librarianship to be published by the American Library Association in 1979 will also include biographical articles, mostly of American and British librarians and library supporters, including some living.

B   8   *Dictionary of national biography from the earliest times to 1900* Oxford University Press, 1908-1909, 22 vols.
Twentieth century supplements 1901-1960. Oxford University Press, 1920-1971, 6 vols; in progress.

The foundation volumes of the *DNB* were kinder to librarians than its twentieth century supplements. For example, it was once a passport to the *DNB* to have been one of Bodley's librarians; it is no longer so. Thus, Sir Edmund Craster (1879-1959), who was not only Bodley's librarian but the Bodleian's historian, is absent. So is Sir John Ballinger (1860-1933), the first librarian of the National Library of Wales. Librarians of local public libraries have no place at all, but Sir Charles Hagberg Wright (1863-1940), librarian of the London Library, has a place. The *DNB* has neither a subject nor a topographical index. There is a subject index to the *Concise dictionary of national biography* Part II 1901-1950 (OUP, 1961), but it is so badly compiled that it conceals such few librarians as are represented.

B   9   *Who was who* 1897-1970. A C Black, 1920-1972, 6 vols; in progress.

Although the entries in *Who was who* (which are based on the final entries for their subjects in *Who's who*) are terse, they include quite a number of librarians, most of whom have not been, or will not be included in the supplements to the *DNB*.

B   10   *Who's who in librarianship* edited by Thomas Landau. Cambridge: Bowes & Bowes, 1954.
           Who's who in librarianship and information science edited by Thomas Landau. 2nd edition, Abelard-Schuman, 1972.

Short biographical entries, based on questionnaires; mostly of British and Commonwealth librarians. There are some notable absentees.

A   11   *Dictionary of American library biography* edited by Bohdan S Wynar. Littleton, Colo; Libraries Unlimited, 1978.

This is far and away the most thorough, authoritative and readable reference work on library history yet published. Over 200 carefully chosen contributors have written lucid and informative biographical essays (up to 6,000 words) on 302 notable Americans who, in some way or other, have made a significant contribution to library progress. Each article ends with a full list of publications about the biographee and notes on relevant archive collections.

Within its necessary limitations, the articles in this *Dictionary* are often extremely good. (See, for example, Phyllis Dain on John Shaw Billings.) The only legitimate reservation which can be made about the work as a whole is that the index of personal names is not enough. A detailed index of subjects and places would be well worth having, even as a separate volume.

The *Dictionary* covers notabilities who died before July 1976. Supplementary sketches will be published in the *Journal of library history*.

A   12   *Dictionary of American biography* New York: Scribner, 1928-1937. 20 vols, plus index volume; reprinted 1946 in 11 vols.
Supplements, Scribner 1944-1974, 4 vols.

A scholarly work with the advantage of a dictionary of occupations, which identifies librarians. These are quite well represented, but the scope of the *Dictionary of American library biography* is wider.

A   13   *Who's who in library service* New York: H W Wilson, 1933; 2nd edition, New York: H W Wilson, 1943; 3rd edition, New York: Grolier Society, 1955; 4th edition, New York: Grolier Society, 1966. Succeeded by:
A biographical directory of librarians in the United States and Canada edited by Lee Ash and B A Uhlendorf. 5th edition, Chicago: American Library Association, 1970.

A cryptic biographical dictionary of the *Who's who* type.

Periodicals
B   14   *Library history* Library Association Library History Group. vol 1 no 1, Spring 1967, to date. Twice a year.

News, articles, signed reviews and an occasional list of British theses on library history and an occasional survey of new library history publications issued in all the countries of Europe. The articles, sometimes illustrated, are mostly on British topics.

Within its restricted space, *Library history* has not been able to diversify as much as the *Journal of library history*, but its coverage of British library history is remarkably wide and it has given a welcome opportunity to many young library historians. Nowadays, however, the longer articles on library history are more likely to be published in the Library Association's quarterly *Journal of librarianship*.

A   15   *Journal of library history, philosophy and comparative librarianship* Tallahassee, Florida: Florida State University Library School. vol 1 no 1, January 1966 to vol 11 no 4, October 1976; University of Texas Press, vol 12 no 1, winter 1977 to date. Quarterly. *Cumulative index* vols 1-11, 1966-1976, University of Texas Press, 1978.

Commonly referred to as the *Journal of library history*, or *JLH*. More substantial, and less insular, than *Library history*. News, articles and signed reviews. An important but irregular feature is 'The year's (or years') work in American library history' (see item 23).

G   16   *Library history review.* Calcutta: K K Roy (Private) Ltd, for the international Agency for Research in Library History. vol 1 no 1, Autumn 1978 to date. Quarterly.

At the time of writing, this journal had not commenced publication. Its declared aim is to provide 'the channel of communication for a world wide net-work of people interested in establishing a library historiography of a high standard of scholarship'.

Bibliographies of library history
B   17   Ollé, James G *Library history: an examination guidebook* 2nd edition, Bingley, 1971.

A critical narrative guide to the major published sources of information on British library history, with a brief survey of the literature on American library history in the final chapter. Intended primarily for students of library history in the British schools of librarianship.

B   18   *British library history: bibliography 1962-1968* edited by Denis F Keeling. Library Association, 1972; *1969-1972,* 1975; *1973-1976,* 1979. In progress.

The volumes of this classified, annotated bibliography, compiled by members of the Library History Group of the Library Association, are probably exhaustive in their coverage of significant publications. They are helpfully arranged, with numerous cross-references, and indexed separately by authors and subjects. The entries for books cite the reviews of them.

The *BLHB* is a splendid work whose merits and value are not yet fully appreciated. For a full assessment see the reviews of the first two volumes by James G Ollé in *Library history* 2 (6) Autumn 1972, 253-255 and 3 (6) Autumn 1975, 204-206.

B   19   'Library history' *in British librarianship and information science 1971-1975* edited by H A Whatley. Library Association, 1977.

This critical survey, by P A Hoare, former editor of *Library history*, deals with the main contributions to the literature on British library history for the period 1971-1975. This is the first time library history has been given a chapter in the LA's 'five years' work' series. Presumably, it will not be the last.

G   20   'Reviews' and 'Notes on other recent publications' *in Library history* vol 1 no 1, Spring 1967 to date.

The review section of *Library history* is often followed by a narrative survey of books and articles on the library history of Britain and the other countries of Europe published in recent months. This item is placed here as the British section is the most comprehensive. Together with the signed reviews, it up-dates the *British library history bibliography.* But see also item 21.

G   21   *ABHB : annual bibliography of the history of the printed book and libraries* 1970 to date. The Hague: Nijhoff. vol 1, 1973, to date.

This bibliography is mainly devoted to the history of printing and publishing, but one section is devoted to 'Institutions. libraries, librarianship, scholarship'. The entries on library history are selective and unannotated. The entries for books cite reviews. Arrangement is by country. The section on Great Britain also serves to up-date the *British library history bibliography*, although it is much in arrears.

A   22   *American library history: a bibliography* edited by Michael H Harris and Donald G Davis Jr. Austin, Texas, University of Texas Press. 1978.

A classified bibliography of 3260 unannotated items on American library history, representing 'the most important literature relating to the historical development of American libraries published through 1976'. Each of the thirteen sections is headed by a short introduction commenting on the works of special significance noted in that section. Updated by the 'Year's work in American library history' (item 23).

A   23   'The year's work in American library history' *in Journal of library history* vol 3 no 4, October 1968, to date.

This narrative critical survey may cover the publications and doctoral dissertations of one year or several years. The record so far is as follows:

'The year's work — 1967' *JLH* 3 (4) October 1968, 342-352.

'The year's work — 1968' *JLH* 5 (2) April 1970, 133-145.

'Two years' work — 1969-1970' *JLH* 7 (1) January 1972, 33-49.

'Three years' work — 1971-1974' *JLH* 9 (4) October 1974, 296-317.

'Two years' work — 1974-1975' *JLH* 11 (4) October 1976, 276-296.

'The year's work — 1976' *JLH* 13 (2) Spring 1978, 187-203.

These surveys have been written singly, or jointly, by Michael H Harris and Donald G Davis.

A   24   'American library history' *in The ALA yearbook: a review of library events* 1976 to date. Chicago: American Library Association, 1977 to date.

This short article is more of a record of library history activities than a bibliographical survey, but it has some bibliographical value.

A   25   Harris, Michael H *A guide to research in American library history* 2nd edition Metuchen, NJ: Scarecrow Press, 1974.

A classified, annotated bibliography of graduate research in American library history 1908-1973, with author and subject indexes. Covers masters' theses and doctoral dissertations. The bibliography is preceded by three chapters on American library history, namely, 'The state of the art', 'Philosophy and methodology for research' 'A guide to the sources'. In the first edition (1968) the bibliography covered the period 1908-1965.

There is no comparable bibliography on British library history theses, but an annotated list of newly accepted theses is published occasionally in *Library history*.

General bibliographies of librarianship
These are listed here as the bibliographies of library history are not yet complete in their coverage. Furthermore, the general bibliographies are essential when searching for source materials.

G   26   Burton, Margaret and Marion E Vosburgh *A bibliography of librarianship* Library Association, 1934; reprinted New York: Burt Franklin, 1970.

A classified, annotated guide to the world literature of librarianship. Includes entries for the older works on library history, such as those of Edward Edwards, and for textbooks and reports which have now become of historical interest.

G   27   Cannons, H G T *Bibliography of library economy. . .
           1876 to 1920* Chicago: American Library Assoc-
           iation, 1927.

This durable but imperfect foundation of the bibliography of
librarianship is often referred to simply as *Cannons*. H G T
Cannons (c 1871-1935) was James Duff Brown's deputy at
Islington, London, and succeeded him as borough librarian.
Cannons is a classified bibliography of librarianship and allied
subjects, based largely on the contents of sixty-five British
and American periodicals and yearbooks. The commencing
date is 1876, as it was in that year that the first periodical
on librarianship was published, namely, the *American library
journal* (soon afterwards renamed the *Library journal*).

  Cannons picks up more articles in non-library periodicals
(such as *Harper's weekly* and the *Studio*) than is generally
realised, although its coverage in this respect is by no means
complete.   Also, its citations are not always absolutely
correct. (See Stuart J Glogoff 'Cannons' *Bibliography of
Library Economy* and its role in the development of bibliographical tools in librarianship' *Journal of library history* 12
(1) winter 1977, 57-63.) Until recently, however, the major
disability of *Cannons* was the lack of an author index. This
has now been remedied by:

G   28   Jordan, Anne Harwell and Melbourne Jordan
           *Cannons' bibliography of library economy 1876-
           1920 : an author index with citations* Metuchen
           NJ: Scarecrow Press, 1976.

This index is a great boon. It not only rapidly identifies the
writings of prolific author-librarians, such as James Duff
Brown, but brings to light the slender contributions to the
literature of librarianship by librarians one might have
supposed to have written nothing at all. The compilers claim
to have corrected a number of *Cannons's* errors, but unfortunately they have followed *Cannons* in citing periodical
articles by volume and page number only, not by date.
Also, some authors appear under more than one heading,
eg 'Milam, C H' and Milam, Carl H'.

  For a brief history of *Cannons* see the review of this
author index to it by W A Munford: *Library Association*

record 79 (3) March 1977, 151-152. *Cannons* has been supplemented by:

G   29   *Library literature 1921-1932* Chicago: American Library Association, 1934.
         Library literature 1933 to date. New York: H W Wilson, 1936 to date. Six issues per annum; annual and multi-annual cumulations.
Alphabetical author and subject index to books, pamphlets and periodical articles on librarianship, mostly American and British. The publications specifically on library history are better covered, within their periods, by the separately published bibliographies of library history (see items 18 and 22); but *Library literature*, like *Cannons*, is invaluable as a bibliography of primary and secondary source materials for research in library history.

G   30   *Library science abstracts* 1950-1968. Library Association, 1950-1969. 19 vols. Quarterly.
International in coverage. Broadly classified, with author and name/subject indexes, annual and also cumulative for vols 2-6, 7-11, 12-16. *LSA* has been continued by:

G   31   *Library and information science abstracts* 1969 to date. Library Association, 1969 to date. Six issues per annum.
Wider in its coverage and with a more sophisticated classification than *Library science abstracts*. Author and subject indexes. In *LISA*, as in *LSA*, items of historical interest are scattered by topic.

G   32   *Year's work in librarianship* 1928-1950. Library Association, 1929-1954. 17 vols. (The war years, 1939-1945, were covered by one volume.)
         Five years' work in librarianship, 1951-1955, 1956-1960, 1961-1965, Library Association, 1958-1968, 3 vols.
         British librarianship and information science 1966-1970, 1971-1975, Library Association, 1972, 1977; in progress.

96

Although all these documented reviews of library progress are of potential value in library history research, especially on modern British library history, there was no specific section devoted to progress in library history itself until the volume covering the period 1971-1975.

G 33 Danton, J Periam *Index to Festschriften in librarianship* New York: Bowker, 1970.
Alphabetical author and subject index to Festschriften published separately, or in journals, throughout the world, form 1864-1966. Thirty-two are from the USA; only six from Great Britain.

B 34 *Radials bulletin* Library Association, 1974 to date. Twice a year.
Radials is an acronym for 'research and development: information and library science'. The *Bulletin* is a detailed, classified list of current research in Great Britain on all aspects of librarianship and information science, with indexes of personal names, organisations, and subjects. A research project is entered repeatedly until the work on it has been completed. Owing to the vagaries of the subject index, the only sure way of identifying historical projects is through page-by-page scrutiny.

Library catalogues
G 35 Library Association *Catalogue of the library* Library Association, 1958.
A catalogue of the books, pamphlets and periodicals in the former Library Association Library, now the British Library Library Association Library, arranged by the Decimal Classification. There is a full author index, but only a highly selective subject index, published as a loose two-page inset.

G 36 *CABLIS* British Library Reference Division, Library Association Library. September 1975 to date. Monthly.
A current awareness bulletin whose primary purpose is to encourage the use of the LA Library. Includes notes on new books, a classified list of additions and abstracts of theses.

G   37   Columbia University. School of Library Service
Dictionary catalog of the library Boston, Mass:
G K Hall, 1962.
Reduced facsimiles of approximately 128,000 catalogue
cards, covering accessions up to 1962.

SEVEN

PREPARING A TEXT FOR SUBMISSION

IN THE preceding chapters I have surveyed the main areas of library history and indicated how they may be explored. For the benefit of those readers who have an ambition to write on some aspect of library history, either for publication, or as some kind of academic exercise, a few words on routine matters such as the gathering and organisation of data and the compilation of notes and references, bibliographies and indexes, may be in order.

I have not discussed in this chapter the actual writing of the text, partly because I have dealt with this incidentally in earlier chapters, and partly because excellent advice is available in two standard manuals written for the guidance of students working in the respective fields of British history and English literature, namely: G Kitson Clark *Guide for research students working on historical subjects* (2nd edition Cambridge University Press, 1968) and George Watson *The literary thesis : a guide to research* (Longman, 1970). The former, a popular and inexpensive pamphlet written by an eminent historian, initially for the guidance of research students working on historical subjects in the University of Cambridge, is worth buying and marking up, as it is replete with sage observations and advice which I can neither challenge nor augment, only endorse. George Watson's manual, which is intended for graduate research workers in English and American literature, although less useful as a whole, is recommended for its chapters on composition, the use of evidence, quotations and references, and style. Particularly good is the essay by R B McKerrow on 'Form and matter in the publication of research' which is reprinted as one of the appendices.

99

Anyone with a major project in hand will also find something to his advantage in a standard American manual, Jacques Barzun and Henry F Graff *The modern researcher* (2nd edition, New York: Harcourt Brace Jovanovich, 1977).

A practical manual which is strongly commended to all researchers in library history is the *MHRA style book*, edited by A S Maney and R L Smallwood (2nd edition Modern Humanities Research Association, 1978); first published in 1971 and several times reprinted. In addition to providing general guidance from the preparation of the typescript to publication, this excellent manual includes a section on the presentation of theses and dissertations and details of proof correction marks, as approved by the British Standards Institution (1976).

Organising the research

There is not much to be said about method, other than to say there should be one. It would be idle to suppose that there is any one method which is suitable for all researchers in library history, or even that one method is necessarily suitable for all the research activities of one particular person.

My own work is supported by a paraphernalia of paper and manilla folders which I think of as 'scaffolding'. It consists of four parts: 1) a chronology file; 2) a set of tentative chapter or topic files; 3) a box of ruled catalogue cards and 4) various charts and other memory aids which are displayed on the walls of my office or study.

The chronology file consists of a set of duplicated A4 sheets divided into a number of named boxes. Thus, for a biography there will be a duplicated sheet for every year of the subject's working life and sheets covering blocks of years for the rest. A blank sheet will look something like the illustration opposite.

As information is discovered, it is copied, or abstracted, for the chapter files and briefly summarised on the chronology sheets. The point of this exercise is that one can seldom follow absolutely a strict chronological order in the text, especially in an extended piece of work.

Furthermore, to avoid the kind of history which Ernest A Savage described as 'gritty with facts and dates', one must

year(s)	age
post held	
offices held	
Professional events	Inf obtained from
Personal events	Inf obtained from
Publications	

decide at the writing stage which facts to withhold or, out of further kindness to the reader, to express in excusably general terms, such as 'by the end of the summer', or 'five years later'. But a detailed chronology must be available to sustain one's work at the writing stage. Without it, some significant matters may be overlooked; for example, the unusual speed with which the Public Libraries Bill 1919 passed through both Houses of Parliament and received the Royal Assent.

Finally, under the organisational heading, an earnest piece of advice. Remember to log full bibliographical details for all notes taken and also (what is more easily overlooked) for all photocopies made or commissioned. Invariably it happens that defective notes are those made in a library far away from home which cannot conveniently be revisited.

Turning now to G Kitson Clark's pamphlet, under the heading 'Presenting the evidence' he says: 'It is not only necessary that your work should be based on critical use of evidence, but you must so present it that the reader can judge upon what evidence it is based.' This points to the vital necessity to support the text of a history with the apparatus of notes, references and a bibliography. In addition, a substantial monograph should be equipped with an index, or indexes.

Notes and references
For publication, notes and references may have to be thinned out (unless your publisher is a university press); but in theses and dissertations they are encouraged to the point where one single sentence may be decorated (if that is the right word) with several superscript numerals.

The location of notes and references, if it is within the author's discretion, is a problem in itself. They may be placed at the bottoms of pages, as footnotes; at the ends of the individual chapters; or all together, at the end of the text. Probably the best solution, if the typist can cope with it, is to put notes and references at the foot of each page. If this is not favoured, or possible, I recommend the end of the text, on the grounds that it is easier to locate the end of the text than it is to locate the ends of chapers. Furthermore, there are some readers (myself among them) who like wholesale browsing among references, in the hope of picking up some hitherto unknown sources of information.

It should be remembered that all information given in notes should be picked up by the index, if there is one. On this matter, as on others, Thomas Kelly's books are exemplary.

Bibliographies
As this is a manual on library history, the observations on the compilation of bibliographies which follow may seem out of place, but I make no apology for them. As a lecturer in subject bibliography, as well as in library history, I have long been aware that the knowledge and skills imparted in one course at a school of librarianship are often regarded by the students (and even by the staff) as relevnt to that subject only, and of no relevance to any other.

Now even in Great Britain, which was laggard in the development of full-time library education, most librarians have either graduated, or are in the process of graduating, from a library school and are, therefore, one would suppose well grounded in librarianship's fundamental disciplines. Nevertheless, when it comes to the compilation and presentation of bibliographies, except when they have specific and binding instructions from editors, publishers, or academic supervisers, librarians can be as infuriatingly negligent as anyone. Bibliography has been described as 'a thankless craft or sullen art'. This was not said by a librarian, but I fear some librarians believe it.

Imagination can be a dangerous gift when used in the service of the muse of history; but, like some potent drugs, it can be extraordinarily beneficial when dispensed in small doses, especially when it enables the historian to project himself into the minds of his intended readers. Will they really understand what he is trying to say with 'no possible doubt whatever'? Will this understanding apply to the work in all its parts, including its 'Further readings', 'List of sources', or whatever it is called? Perhaps not. In my experience, frequently not.

S R Ranganathan's so-called 'Five laws of library science' are probably regarded by many librarians as part of the dross of library science. One of his laws, however, can be a useful slogan for librarians engaged in bibliographical work: 'Save the time of the reader'. The potential usefulness of this 'law' is considerable. Borne firmly in mind by a library historian it will prevent him making such crass mistakes as referring to an author as the author would never have referred to himself (eg Sir F Kenyon, instead of Sir Frederic); from citing the non-descriptive title of a book, but suppressing its descriptive sub-title; from stating where a book is published but not the name of the publisher; and from using abbreviations which are ambiguous, such as Inst, or not common currency, such as RHS (Royal Historical Society).

Truly, there are no depths to which librarians will not sink when they try to be bibliographers. They will even use 'nd', a vile abbreviation whose meaning, properly interpreted, is 'I have seen this book and I know that it was published somewhere between Gutenberg and this year of grace, but beyond that I cannot go'.

Unhappily, all these faults are displayed in two standard works on library history mentioned earlier; namely, Raymond Irwin's volume of essays *The English library: sources and history* (Allen & Unwin, 1966) and the well-known American textbook Elmer D Johnson and Michael H Harris *History of libraries in the western world* (3rd edition Metuchen NJ, Scarecrow Press, 1976).

The 'List of sources' at the end of Irwin's book extends to five and a half pages. About 150 titles are listed, in alphabetical order of author. Typical entries are:

Bevan, E R and C Singer *The legacy of Israel* 1927.

Ducket, E *The wandering saints* 1959.

Gunther, R T *Early British botanists and their gardens* 1922.

In Johnson and Harris, in lieu of a general bibliography there are lists of 'Additional readings' appended to the chapters. Some of the lists are quite long; but here, also, the order is alphabetical by author. Specimen entries:

Harding, T S *College literary societies* Brooklyn, 1971.

Kraus, J W 'The book collections of early American college libraries', *Library quarterly* 43 (1973): 142-59.

Shores L *Origins of the American college library, 1638-1800* New York, 1935.

If it seems to you that there is nothing wrong with these entries, or with the arrangement of the bibliographies from which they have been extracted, take note of what follows.

Unhelpful arrangement

Robert L Collison has said: 'There is something very satisfying in handling a well-constructed bibliography: the care and enthusiasm with which the bibliographer has applied himself to his task is reflected in the thoughtful annotations, the ample cross-references and the careful selection of material, so that the user is continually being directed to new and unsuspected resources, his mind stimulated by new ideas and his conception of his subject enriched by the indications of new fields as yet unexplored.'(1)

Clearly, what Mr Collison had in mind were the select bibliographies which are guides, rather than the great reference bibliographies which are merely aids. The arrangement

of bibliographies is always important. In a reference bibliography of the H W Wilson type, alphabetical order has its
merits. In the type of bibliography we are considering, which
is intended to direct someone's studies, it is pointless. A
good select bibliography should tell a story; and when
appended to a treatise the story should be not only what
sources of information the author consulted and found
useful, but why he found them useful.

If you were to write a monograph on, say, public library
development in Great Britain since 1945, and for this exercise, when writing the chapter on children's libraries you
used six books and twenty-three periodical articles, why
should you merge these twenty-nine items with the other
187 you used for the rest of the work and surrender the
entire 216 to the heartless tyranny of the alphabet? Common sense suggests there should be a breakdown; first by
subject, then by physical form, as when applying a bibliography to the stock of a library it is an advantage to have
books and pamphlets listed separately from periodical
articles.

Imperfect bibliographical descriptions
The lack of common sense and imagination which often
spoils the arrangement of bibliographies, wreaks even greater
havoc in the description of individual items, as the entries
transcribed above from Irwin, and Johnson and Harris,
show only too well. The common faults are these:

1 The use of an initial where the author commonly uses
his forename in full, or vice versa. The reader should not
have to pause and speculate whether 'L Shores' is the well-
known 'Louis Shores', or 'Kenneth Cecil Harrison' is the
familiar 'K C Harrison'.

2 The suppression of publishers' names and/or places of
publication is particularly aggravating. It suggests that the
bibliographer's attitude is: 'I, who am a learned, well-read
person, know one publisher from another. You, dear reader,
I suspect do not. Furthermore, it matters to me, and to the
staffs of the libraries and bookshops I use, whether a book is
published in London, New York, Toronto, or Sydney, but
I cannot think of any reason why this information should
be of any use to you.'

3) The lack of precise details of periodical articles can be tiresome, also. They should always include the volume number, issue number, the precise date of the issue, and the full pagination. If this seems extravagant, consider: if a library files a periodical, it may bind it or keep it unbound. If it binds it, the bound volumes may have only the volume numbers on the spines, or only the years (strange but true). Therefore, to have a reference which gives both saves time, and one piece of information is a check on the other. If the periodical is unbound, the identification of one particular issue, particularly of a weekly, would be easier and quicker using the issue number than the date. It would certainly be so for the *Times literary supplement*. As to pagination, usage such as 142+ is stupid and 142-59 is slovenly, and even likely to puzzle some readers.

The bibliography in Irwin's book includes a reference to a very important article, by Frank Beckwith, as follows:

Beckwith, F., 'Eighteenth Century Proprietary Libraries', *J of Documentation*, 1947, III, p 85.

For maximum helpfulness to readers, this entry should read as follows:

Beckwith, Frank 'The eighteenth century proprietary library in England' *Journal of documentation* 3(2) September 1947 p 85.

Even this is unsatisfactory, however, as it is not clear why Irwin recommended only one page of this important article instead of all of it (81-98). This brings us to another vital aspect of bibliographical work: annotations and abstracts.

Annotations and abstracts
An annotation for every book, and an abstract of every article, would greatly increase the labour of compiling a bibliography and the cost of typing it; perhaps the cost of printing it, also. But some items cry aloud for annotation and, therefore, should have it. But here let me preach the gospel of *relevance*. If, for example, you have written a study of the libraries of the Mechanics' Institutes of Great Britain during the Victorian period and you include in your bibliography Richard D Altick *The English common reader: a social history of the mass reading public 1800-1900* (Chicago:

106

University of Chicago Press, 1957) you had better add a note explaining that it not only includes useful background information on education, literacy, publishing and book-selling, which may be guessed from the sub-title, but sections (which should be identified) on the Institutes themselves.

Why did Raymond Irwin list R T Gunther's *Early British botanists and their gardens*? Why did Johnson and Harris list T S Harding's *College literary societies*? I do not know and I grudge the time I would have to expend to find out.

At the very least, all books (and articles) with non-descriptive titles should carry explanatory notes, unless they have descriptive sub-titles which will serve, eg Charles T Laugher *Thomas Bray's grand design: libraries of the Church of England in America 1695-1785* (Chicago: American Library Association, 1973).

Indexes

Two problems arise here: 'Should there be an index?' and 'What kind of an index should it be?' As to the first question, the authors of theses often neglect to provide indexes, as well as other useful aids, such as page headings. They, therefore, hinder other research workers, who will want to find out, as quickly as possible, if there is anything in the text relevant to their own studies.

As to the kind of index, it must be fully informative. If observation and common sense do not help, there is no lack of reputable manuals on indexing. Common faults are the lack of cross-references, cascades of bare page numbers (eg New York Public Library 23, 27, 31, 35, 39-41, 47 etc) and infuriating entries such as:

Circulating libraries *See under the names of individual libraries*

If it is desirable that every librarian should be proficient in report writing, and have what I call bibliographical literacy, library history provides as much scope for profitable exercise as any area of library science.

Let the last word be with G Kitson Clark. He said that the goal of the historian is 'to produce an interesting, readable, lucid and significant piece of work'. This chapter has dealt with some of the matters which come under the heading 'lucid', which means 'easily understood'.

NOTES AND REFERENCES

CHAPTER 1 : *Introduction—the state of the art*
1 Irwin, Raymond *The English library* Allen & Unwin, 1966, 19.
2 Munford, W A 'Our library inheritance' *Library review* 17 (130) Summer 1959, 102.
3 Krzys, Richard 'Library historiography' in *Encyclopedia of library and information science* New York: Marcel Dekker, vol 15, 1975, 294-330.
4 Munford, W A 'Confessions of a library biographer' *Library review* 21 (6) Summer 1968, 294.

CHAPTER 2 : *Time, place, type of library, type of activity*
1 Thompson, James Westfall (ed) *The medieval library* Chicago: Chicago University Press, 1939; reprinted New York: Hafner, 1957.
McCrimmon, Barbara *Anthony Panizzi as administrator* University of Illinois Library School Occasional Papers 65, 1963.
McCrimmon, Barbara 'Nineteenth century swingers: the movable press at the British Museum' *Library review* 25 (3-4) Autumn-Winter 1975-1976, 119-123.
Griest, Guinevere L *Mudie's Circulating Library and the Victorian novel* Bloomington: Indiana University Press, 1970; Newton Abbot: David & Charles, 1971.
2 Humphreys K W *The book provisions of the mediaeval friars 1215-1400* Amsterdam: Erasmus Booksellers, 1964.
3 Chesterton, G K *A short history of England* Chatto & Windus, 1917, 2-3.
4 Irwin, Raymond *The English library* Allen & Unwin, 1966, 80.

5 Knowles, David *The monastic order in England* Cambridge University Press, 1940, 522.

6 Ollé, James G *Ernest A Savage : librarian extraordinary* Library Association, 1977, 65-67.

7 *The Leeds Library 1768-1968* Leeds: Leeds Library, 1968, 11. Published anonymously, but almost certainly the work of Frank Beckwith, formerly librarian of the Leeds Library.

8 Kelly, Thomas *George Birkbeck: pioneer of adult education* Liverpool: Liverpool University Press, 1957, 257-258.

9 The archives of the American Library Association are now in the care of the University Archivist, University of Illinois at Urbana-Champaign. They are briefly described by Maynard Brichford in 'Current status of the American Library Association archives: a preliminary report' *Journal of library history* 12 (1) Winter 1977, 64-65.

CHAPTER 3 : *The individual library*

1 Kelly, Thomas *History of public libraries in Great Britain 1845-1975* 2nd revised edition, Library Association, 1977, v.

2 Kelly, Thomas *Early public libraries* Library Association, 1966, 244-266.
Kaufman, Paul 'The community library: a chapter in English social history' *Transactions of the American Philosophical Society* ns 57 (7) October 1967, 50-54.

3 A good recent example of the history of a library written by one of its own librarians is S P L Filon *The National Central Library: an experiment in library co-operation* Library Association, 1977. Mr Filon was Librarian and Secretary to the Trustees of the former NCL 1958-1971.

4 This observation was suggested by John Cowell 'The rise and fall of the free public library movement in Marylebone, 1850-1860' *Library history* 3 (4) Autumn 1974, 140-146. This is based on part of Mr Cowell's master's thesis on the long fight for a public library service in Marylebone. (Loughborough University of Technology, 1972).

5 Cardus, [Sir] Neville *Autobiography* Collins, 1947, 22-23.

6 Ollé, James G 'Reference library statistics' *RQ* 3 (3) January 1964, 5.

7 Kelly, Thomas 'Thoughts on the writing of library history' *Library history* 3 (5) Spring 1975, 168.

8 Marshall, J D 'Leadership needed to make local libraries more respectable' *Times higher educational supplement* March 19th 1978, 10.

9 Kelly Thomas From a taped interview with David E Gerard, College of Librarianship, Wales, 1975.

10 Abbott, John C 'Review of *Parnassus on Main Street* by Frank B Woodford' *College and research libraries* 27 (4) July 1966, 318.

CHAPTER 4 : *The biographical approach*

1 Holroyd, Michael 'About chaps' *The Times* September 14th 1974, 9.

2 McCrimmon, Barbara 'Review of *Prince of librarians* by Edward J Miller' *Journal of library history* 3 (3) 1968, 272-275.

3 The library biographies of Dr W A Munford are as follows:

William Ewart MP 1798-1869 : portrait of a radical Grafton, 1960.

Edward Edwards 1812-1886 : portrait of a librarian Library Association, 1963.

James Duff Brown 1862-1914 : portrait of a library pioneer Library Association, 1968.

The following biography was a collaboration:

Fry, W G and W A Munford *Louis Stanley Jast : a biographical sketch* Library Association, 1966.

4 Munford, W A 'Confessions of a library biographer' *Library review* 21 (6) Summer 1968, 296.

5 Holroyd, Michael *op cit* 9.

6 Garrison, Fielding H *John Shaw Billings : a memoir* New York: Putnam, 1915, 195, 300. W A Munford was fortunate, also, when he wrote his biography of Edward Edwards, as he was able to draw upon several volumes of Edwards's diary.

7 Savage, Ernest A 'Letter to the editor' *Library world* 60 (707) May 1959, 250.

8 Holley, Edward G 'Review of *William Frederick Poole and the modern library movement* by William Landram Williamson' *College and research libraries* 25 (2) March 1964, 155.

9 J C Kennedy is currently engaged on a master's thesis, on the life and work of Miss A S Cooke, Loughborough University of Technology, probable completion date 1979.

10 The career of J T Houghton is chronicled by Mrs D J Thomas in her master's thesis *Libraries of Worksop 1830-1939* Loughborough University of Technology, 1978, 34-88.

11 Wiegand, Wayne A 'The wayward bookman : the decline, fall and historical obliteration of an ALA President' *American libraries* 8 (3-4) March-April 1977, 134-137, 197-200.

12 On the strange career of Henry Bond see the complementary articles by James G Ollé 'A librarian of no importance' *Library review* 22 (6) Summer 1970, 291-298; and 'Prayers at Highgate' *Library review* 21 (7) Autumn 1968, 351-356.

13 There was a passing reference to a notorious chairman of Leeds City Libraries Committee in 'This librarian's librarian' *Library Association record* 80 (1) January 1978, 4. There is a much fuller reference to him in the taped interview between the late F G B Hutchings and David E Gerard; College of Librarianship, Wales, 1974.

CHAPTER 7 : *Preparing a text for submission*
1 Collison, Robert L *Bibliographies: subject and national* 3rd Edition, Crosby Lockwood, 1968, xiii.

INDEX

Books and articles only casually referred to in the text are not entered in the index. The abbreviation 'lh' means 'library history'.

Danton, J Periam, *Index to Fest-schriften in librarianship* 97
Davis, Donald G: *American library history: a bibliography* 8-9, 93; 'Year's work in American library history' 94
Dictionary of American biography 90
Dictionary of American library biography (DALB) 62-3, 89-90
Dictionary of national biography 88-9
dissertations on lh *see under* theses
Ditzion, Sidney: on public library history 17, 51; *Arsenals of a democratic culture* 17

editing reprints 77-8
Edwards, Edward: biography of 15, 111; life and writings 12-13
Ellis, Alec, *Library services for young people 1830-1970* 41
Elton, G R, on the value of history 25-6
Encyclopedia of library and information science 86-8

Festschriften in librarianship, bibliography of 97
Five years' work in librarianship 96

Garrison, Fielding H, *John Shaw Billings: a memoir* 65-6
Gerard, David, work on oral history 79
Harris, Michael H: on interest in lh 20; on American lh 21; on lh theses 19, 21; *A guide to research in American library history* 21, 94; *American library history: a bibliography* 8-9, 93; *History of libraries in the western world* 31, 104; editor 'Heritage of librarianship' series' 65
Held, Ray E, trilogy on Californian lh 31
history, value of 24-6
history of libraries *see* library history
Holley, Edward G, on librarians' private papers 67
Holroyd, Michael. on the art of biography 61, 64
Houghton, J T, role in Worksop experiment 67-8

humour in lh 23-4
Hutchings, F G B: obituary notice of 72; on Septimus Pitt 71-2

illustrations on lh 81-2
industrial special libraries 38
Irwin, Raymond: defence of lh 11; on ancient lh 33-4; writings on lh 15, 34

Jast, Louis Stanley: fragment of autobiography 74; unknown essay on public libraries 84
Jefferson, George, *Library co-operation* 41
Johnson, Elmer D, *History of libraries in the western world* 31, 104
Jordan, Anne Harwell and Melbourne Jordan, *Cannons' bibliography of library economy...an author index* 95
Journal of library history 18, 83, 91

Kaufman, Paul, studies of British lh 46
Kelly, Edith, *Books for the people* 27, 81
Kelly, Thomas: career 15-16; classification of libraries 36; on histories of individual libraries 45-6, 56-8; *Books for the people* 27, 81; *Early public libraries* 16, 36-7; *History of public libraries in Great Britain* 25, 27, 45-6
Kryzs, Richard, on lh 11

librarians: autobiographies 74-5; biographies 62-76; humorous anecdotes of 23
library architecture 42-3
Library Association: neglect of pictorial archives 82; *Catalogue of the library* 97; *History of the Library Association* 15, 43
Library Association Library History Group: foundation and objects 15-16, 47; *Library history* 16, 90-1
library associations, histories of 43
library history: ancient libraries 33; autobiographies 74-5; biblio-graphies 83-4, 91-7, 102-7; bio-graphies 62-76; circulating li-braries 36; (cont)